Approaches to learning and teaching

Mathematics

a toolkit for international teachers

Charlie Gilderdale, Alison Kiddle, Ems Lord, Becky Warren and Fran Watson

Series Editors: Paul Ellis and Lauren Harris

CAMBRIDGE
UNIVERSITY PRESS

University Printing House, Cambridge CB2 8BS, United Kingdom

One Liberty Plaza, 20th Floor, New York, NY 10006, USA

477 Williamstown Road, Port Melbourne, VIC 3207, Australia

4843/24, 2nd Floor, Ansari Road, Daryaganj, Delhi – 110002, India

79 Anson Road, #06–04/06, Singapore 079906

Cambridge University Press is part of the University of Cambridge.

It furthers the University's mission by disseminating knowledge in the pursuit of education, learning and research at the highest international levels of excellence.

www.cambridge.org
Information on this title: www.cambridge.org/9781108406970 (Paperback)

© Cambridge International Examinations 2017

First published 2017

20 19 18 17 16 15 14 13 12 11 10 9 8 7 6 5 4 3 2 1

Printed in Great Britain by CPI Group (UK) Ltd, Croydon CR0 4YY

A catalogue record for this publication is available from the British Library

ISBN 978-1-108-40697-0 Paperback

Contents

Acknowledgements

The authors and publishers acknowledge the following sources of copyright material and are grateful for the permissions granted.

Cover bgblue/Getty Images
Figure 4.1 'Charlie's Delightful Marchine', created by Charlie Gilderdale for NRICH and Figures 4.2–4.4 based on activities by NRICH, copyright of the University of Cambridge, all rights reserved.

Introduction to the series by the editors

1

1 Approaches to learning and teaching Mathematics

This series of books is the result of close collaboration between Cambridge University Press and Cambridge International Examinations, both departments of the University of Cambridge. The books are intended as a companion guide for teachers, to supplement your learning and provide you with extra resources for the lessons you are planning. Their focus is deliberately not syllabus-specific, although occasional reference has been made to programmes and qualifications. We want to invite you to set aside for a while assessment objectives and grading, and take the opportunity instead to look in more depth at how you teach your subject and how you motivate and engage with your students.

The themes presented in these books are informed by evidence-based research into what works to improve students' learning and pedagogical best practices. To ensure that these books are first and foremost practical resources, we have chosen not to include too many academic references, but we have provided some suggestions for further reading.

We have further enhanced the books by asking the authors to create accompanying lesson ideas. These are described in the text and can be found in a dedicated space online. We hope the books will become a dynamic and valid representation of what is happening now in learning and teaching in the context in which you work.

Our organisations also offer a wide range of professional development opportunities for teachers. These range from syllabus- and topic-specific workshops and large-scale conferences to suites of accredited qualifications for teachers and school leaders. Our aim is to provide you with valuable support, to build communities and networks, and to help you both enrich your own teaching methodology and evaluate its impact on your students.

Each of the books in this series follows a similar structure. In the first chapter, we have asked our authors to consider the essential elements of their subject, the main concepts that might be covered in a school curriculum, and why these are important. The next chapter gives you a brief guide on how to interpret a syllabus or subject guide, and how to plan a programme of study. The authors will encourage you to think too about what is not contained in a syllabus and how you can pass on your own passion for the subject you teach.

The main body of the text takes you through those aspects of learning and teaching which are widely recognised as important. We would like to stress that there is no single recipe for excellent teaching, and that different schools, operating in different countries and cultures, will have strong traditions that should be respected. There is a growing consensus, however, about some important practices and approaches that need to be adopted if students are going to fulfil their potential and be prepared for modern life.

In the common introduction to each of these chapters we look at what the research says and the benefits and challenges of particular approaches. Each author then focuses on how to translate theory into practice in the context of their subject, offering practical lesson ideas and teacher tips. These chapters are not mutually exclusive but can be read independently of each other and in whichever order suits you best. They form a coherent whole but are presented in such a way that you can dip into the book when and where it is most convenient for you to do so.

The final two chapters are common to all the books in this series and are not written by the subject authors. Schools and educational organisations are increasingly interested in the impact that classroom practice has on student outcomes. We have therefore included an exploration of this topic and some practical advice on how to evaluate the success of the learning opportunities you are providing for your students. The book then closes with some guidance on how to reflect on your teaching and some avenues you might explore to develop your own professional learning.

We hope you find these books accessible and useful. We have tried to make them conversational in tone so you feel we are sharing good practice rather than directing it. Above all, we hope that the books will inspire you and enable you to think in more depth about how you teach and how your students learn.

Paul Ellis and Lauren Harris

Series Editors

2 | Purpose and context

International research into educational effectiveness tells us that student achievement is influenced most by what teachers do in classrooms. In a world of rankings and league tables we tend to notice performance, not preparation, yet the product of education is more than just examinations and certification. Education is also about the formation of effective learning habits that are crucial for success within and beyond the taught curriculum.

The purpose of this series of books is to inspire you as a teacher to reflect on your practice, try new approaches and better understand how to help your students learn. We aim to help you develop your teaching so that your students are prepared for the next level of their education as well as life in the modern world.

This book will encourage you to examine the processes of learning and teaching, not just the outcomes. We will explore a variety of teaching strategies to enable you to select which is most appropriate for your students and the context in which you teach. When you are making your choice, involve your students: all the ideas presented in this book will work best if you engage your students, listen to what they have to say, and consistently evaluate their needs.

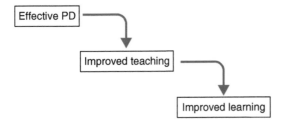

Cognitive psychologists, coaches and sports writers have noted how the aggregation of small changes can lead to success at the highest level. As teachers, we can help our students make marginal gains by guiding them in their learning, encouraging them to think and talk about how they are learning, and giving them the tools to monitor their success. If you take care of the learning, the performance will take care of itself.

When approaching an activity for the first time, or revisiting an area of learning, ask yourself if your students know how to:

- approach a new task and plan which strategies they will use
- monitor their progress and adapt their approach if necessary
- look back and reflect on how well they did and what they might do differently next time.

2 Approaches to learning and teaching Mathematics

Effective learners understand that learning is an active process. We need to challenge and stretch our students and enable them to interrogate, analyse and evaluate what they see and hear. Consider whether your students:

- challenge assumptions and ask questions
- try new ideas and take intellectual risks
- devise strategies to overcome any barriers to their learning that they encounter.

As we discuss in the chapters on **Active learning** and **Metacognition,** it is our role as teachers to encourage these practices with our students so that they become established routines. We can help students review their own progress as well as getting a snapshot ourselves of how far they are progressing by using some of the methods we explore in the chapter on **Assessment for Learning**.

Students often view the subject lessons they are attending as separate from each other, but they can gain a great deal if we encourage them to take a more holistic appreciation of what they are learning. This requires not only understanding how various concepts in a subject fit together, but also how to make connections between different areas of knowledge and how to transfer skills from one discipline to another. As our students successfully integrate disciplinary knowledge, they are better able to solve complex problems, generate new ideas and interpret the world around them.

In order for students to construct an understanding of the world and their significance in it, we need to lead students into thinking habitually about why a topic is important on a personal, local and global scale. Do they realise the implications of what they are learning and what they do with their knowledge and skills, not only for themselves but also for their neighbours and the wider world? To what extent can they recognise and express their own perspective as well as the perspectives of others? We will consider how to foster local and global awareness, as well as personal and social responsibility, in the chapter on **Global thinking**.

As part of the learning process, some students will discover barriers to their learning: we need to recognise these and help students to overcome them. Even students who regularly meet success face their own challenges. We have all experienced barriers to our own learning at some point in our lives and should be able as teachers to empathise and share our own methods for dealing with these. In the chapter on **Inclusive education** we discuss how to make learning accessible for everyone and how to ensure that all students receive the instruction and support they need to succeed as learners.

Some students are learning through the medium of English when it is not their first language, while others may struggle to understand subject jargon even if they might otherwise appear fluent. For all students, whether they are learning through their first language or an additional language, language is a vehicle for learning. It is through language that students access the content of the lesson and communicate their ideas. So, as teachers, it is our responsibility to make sure that language isn't a barrier to learning. In the chapter on **Language awareness** we look at how teachers can pay closer attention to language to ensure that all students can access the content of a lesson.

Alongside a greater understanding of what works in education and why, we as teachers can also seek to improve how we teach and expand the tools we have at our disposal. For this reason, we have included a chapter in this book on **Teaching with digital technologies**, discussing what this means for our classrooms and for us as teachers. Institutes of higher education and employers want to work with students who are effective communicators and who are information literate. Technology brings both advantages and challenges and we invite you to reflect on how to use it appropriately.

This book has been written to help you think harder about the impact of your teaching on your students' learning. It is up to you to set an example for your students and to provide them with opportunities to celebrate success, learn from failure and, ultimately, to succeed.

We hope you will share what you gain from this book with other teachers and that you will be inspired by the ideas that are presented here. We hope that you will encourage your school leaders to foster a positive environment that allows both you and your students to meet with success and to learn from mistakes when success is not immediate. We hope too that this book can help in the creation and continuation of a culture where learning and teaching are valued and through which we can discover together what works best for each and every one of our students.

3 The nature of the subject

Mathematics is a unique subject within the school curriculum. Not only does it underpin many other subject areas, but mathematical truth is fundamentally different from other types of knowledge. Mathematics has a rich and varied history – for as long as people have been reasoning, they have been doing Mathematics. We believe that we have a duty to offer all students the opportunity to engage with rich Mathematics that will allow them to appreciate its unique nature for themselves.

Mathematical truth

Mathematical ideas in some form have existed for thousands of years.

The ancient Greeks were among the first to engage with the sort of thinking that we now recognise as mathematical proof. In ancient Greek society, people spent time debating philosophical ideas. They came to realise that, unlike other types of thought, mathematical truth was resistant to sceptical attack, because once they had proved something, no one else could disprove it. As a consequence, the study of Mathematics became an important part of a classical education. The first proofs were geometrical. Euclid proposed a set of axioms that were widely agreed on, and much of early academic Mathematics consisted of making logical deductions from his starting points in order to prove new theorems.

Humankind has always been fascinated by marking the passage of time. As part of our intrinsic desire to make sense of the world around us, throughout human history we have tried to explain the motion of the stars and planets. We have also taken an interest in scientific questions closer to home, such as why things float, why people get sick, how to build better bridges and how much wine can be held in a barrel. Many developments in the history of Mathematics came about as a result of people needing to explain phenomena, and sharing some of their stories can help to bring Mathematics alive for our students.

Here are some suggestions of historical mathematical figures whose stories might be of interest:

- Archimedes, who solved the problem of working out the density of the king's crown while taking a bath.
- Al-Khwarizmi, who developed methods for solving equations and after whom the word 'algorithm' was named.

- Isaac Newton, who formulated laws that govern motion and gravitational effects, and developed calculus.
- Galileo Galilei, who was imprisoned by the church for expounding the theory of heliocentricity.
- René Descartes, who linked algebra and geometry through his invention of Cartesian coordinates.
- Pierre de Fermat and Blaise Pascal, whose correspondence formed the beginnings of probability theory.

The Mathematics that each of these people did covered a wide range of ideas, but the common thread between them is proof – taking agreed starting points and making deductions to develop new theorems.

If we want our students to work like mathematicians, we need to be explicit about the different types of knowledge seen in a Mathematics classroom. Dave Hewitt introduced the terms 'arbitrary', to refer to that which students need to be told, and 'necessary', that which they can deduce for themselves.

For example, if you draw a shape with four right angles and four equal sides, the fact that it's called a square is 'arbitrary'. Different languages and cultures will use words other than 'square' to describe the same object. However, the fact that its diagonals intersect at 90 degrees is a property of a square that students can discover for themselves – it is a 'necessary' truth. No matter when or where a square is drawn, its diagonals will always have this property. This type of mathematical truth is universal and it is important that students are offered opportunities to appreciate such universality.

Mathematics as a foundation for other subjects

A teacher challenged her students to come up with a job that didn't include any Mathematics at all. One student thought he had cracked this with the suggestion 'priest', but was met with the response 'Who would be responsible for the parish accounts then?' Mathematics is inherent in our daily lives. Whether the context is finance, measurement or making sense of data, students need to be competent and confident in thinking mathematically, in order to live successful lives.

Not only do we want our students to recognise the beauty and truth of Mathematics, we also want to equip them with skills to help them make sense of the world. Students may come into the Mathematics classroom with a passion for Science, Geography, Music, Art or even skateboarding, and this provides us with an opportunity to show them the Mathematics that underpins what they love.

If we want our students to have a well-rounded Mathematics education, we need to give them plenty of experience of doing Mathematics for its own sake, as well as lots of opportunities to apply mathematical thinking to real-world contexts and everyday problem-solving. This balance of pure and applied Mathematics will ensure that our students see Mathematics as useful, worthwhile, interesting and accessible.

As well as sharing stories of pure mathematicians, your students might also be interested to hear about historical figures who used Mathematics in other fields.

- Leonardo da Vinci, artist, inventor, musician, writer…
- Tycho Brahe, who made extremely accurate astronomical observations.
- Isambard Kingdom Brunel, who had visionary ideas about progressing civil engineering in the 19th century.
- Florence Nightingale, who used statistical representations of medical data.

Why not invite your students to research other users of Mathematics in history, to illustrate just how widely the subject has permeated our existence?

Mathematics as a process

We've talked about the nature of mathematical knowledge and the place of Mathematics in relation to other subjects. However, Mathematics can also be considered as a process or set of skills that can be applied in problem-solving contexts.

3

Approaches to learning and teaching Mathematics

Consider the two problems:

'Marbles in a Box' (www.nrich.maths.org/marbles) poses the question: In a three-dimensional version of noughts and crosses, how many winning lines can you make?

'Keep it Simple' (www.nrich.maths.org/keepitsimple) invites students to explore the number of ways in which one-unit fractions can be written as the sum of two different-unit fractions.

$$\frac{1}{6} = \frac{1}{7} + \frac{1}{42}$$

$$\frac{1}{6} = \frac{1}{8} + \frac{1}{24}$$

$$\frac{1}{6} = \frac{1}{9} + \frac{1}{18}$$

$$\frac{1}{6} = \frac{1}{10} + \frac{1}{15}$$

These two problems are taken from very different areas of the curriculum, and at first glance might not seem to have much in common. However, if we consider Mathematics as a way of thinking rather than as a body of knowledge, the two problems are surprisingly similar. Both are concerned with the number of possible solutions to a problem, and both become accessible when students explore the underlying structure.

We often share with students the mathematical content that might be the objective of a particular lesson. This may give the impression that Mathematics IS knowledge. If we also explicitly reference mathematical skills, students can begin to develop their own understanding of what it means to think mathematically.

Here are eight aspects of working mathematically that you may find it helpful to consider:

- exploring and noticing structure
- thinking strategically
- visualising
- representing
- working systematically
- posing questions and making conjectures
- mathematical modelling
- reasoning, convincing and proof.

We will explore these categories in more detail in future chapters.

Summary

The nature of Mathematics can be considered in three broad strands:

- the role of proof in giving mathematical truth a unique status

- the role of Mathematics in supporting other areas of human endeavour

- the processes and skills needed to work mathematically.

A mathematical education that captures all three of these strands has the capacity to convey our excitement about the subject and inspire our students to think like mathematicians.

4 Key considerations

As teachers of Mathematics, there are three key considerations to take into account when planning our lessons. These key considerations need to address students who dislike Mathematics, who lack independence or who are unwilling to use practical resources.

As teachers, we can easily fall into the trap of complaining that students 'can't get started on a problem' or 'they do not like Mathematics'. Our challenge is to turn those comments around, so that students can get started on problems and feel positive about doing and learning Mathematics.

Engaging students

Although Mathematics is a fascinating subject that frequently breaks new ground, pushing the limits of our knowledge and challenging accepted views, many students do not regard it as a dynamic subject. Nevertheless, every lesson offers an opportunity to share our enthusiasm and help students appreciate why so many people find Mathematics such a compelling subject. The following activity offers enormous potential for engaging your students:

☑ LESSON IDEA ONLINE 4.1: CHARLIE'S DELIGHTFUL MACHINE

Many standard questions give just the right amount of information required to solve them. In real life, we often have to sift through information to decide which is the most relevant to solve a given problem. In 'Charlie's Delightful Machine' (www.nrich.maths.org/delightful), students need to go in search of the information and work in a systematic way in order to make sense of the results they gather (see Figure 4.1). They need to try to get all of the lights to switch on, but may discover that it might not always be quite as straightforward as they expect. →

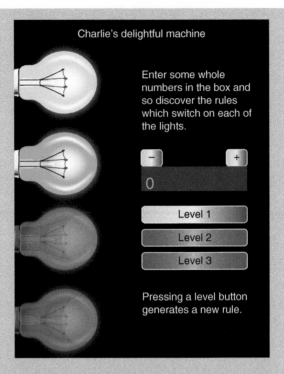

Figure 4.1

Begin the lesson by dividing your board into two columns, one headed with a tick and the other with a cross. Ask students to suggest some numbers, and record each suggestion in the appropriate column according to a rule of your choice. Make it clear to the class that the activity is designed to model scientific enquiry, so they can come up with a hypothesis for your rule, but you will not confirm their hypothesis, only place their numbers in the appropriate column.

Teacher Tip

Here are some suggestions for rules:
- odd numbers
- numbers that are 1 more than multiples of 4
- numbers that are 2 less than multiples of 5
- numbers that are 3 more than multiples of 7.

Once your class have tried the activity with a couple of rules, and are reasonably convinced that their →

hypothesis holds, you can move them on to the main task. Demonstrate the interactive version of the problem, entering a couple of numbers and noting which lights are switched on each time. Make sure that your students understand that more than one light can light up at once, and that each light is governed by its own rule.

Here are some interesting questions that students may ask themselves (or you can encourage them to consider):

1 What is special about rules that light up numbers that:
   - Are all odd?
   - Are all even?
   - Are a mixture of odd and even?
   - Are all multiples of 3? Or 4?
   - Have a last digit of 7?

2 If two lights can be made to switch on together, is there a connection between the rules that light up each individual light and the rule that lights up the pair? Or lights up three at once? Or all four?

3 Sometimes it's impossible to switch a pair of lights on at the same time.

How can you decide when it is impossible?

Multiple representations

Teachers often mistakenly believe that practical resources, such as cubes and number line, are only suitable for lower-attaining students. Nothing could be further from the truth. Students should experience using resources in a variety of ways and have easy access to them in lessons. The effective use of resources allows your students to communicate mathematically, explore alternative approaches to problem-solving and develop as independent students. Many industries make excellent use of modelling to communicate their ideas to a wider audience, such as architecture and aircraft design. All Mathematics classrooms should have a range of easily accessible resources and you should use them frequently in lessons.

▣ LESSON IDEA ONLINE 4.2: FACTORISING WITH MULTILINK

Figure 4.2

When students first meet factorisation, they often don't make the connection between factorising an algebraic expression and breaking a number up into factor pairs. 'Factorising with Multilink' uses a visual representation that allows students to make that connection and discover for themselves the properties necessary for a quadratic expression to factorise. It also relies on a resource that many students initially encountered in their junior school. This activity celebrates the adaptability of resources to support students of all ages and abilities to engage with Mathematics.

To begin this activity, hand out Multilink cubes to your students and ask them to arrange 12 cubes into rectangles. Discuss how the different configurations can be used to illustrate the factors of 12.

In order to introduce the factorisation of algebraic expressions, ask your students to organise themselves into groups of three or four. Select a number base for each group. Using Multilink cubes, give them time to create some squares, sticks and units in their bases. For example, if they are working in base 3 they will need units, sticks of three and squares of nine cubes (see Figure 4.2).

Next, challenge each group to make a rectangle using their different bases. Start by asking them to take 1 square, 3 sticks and 2 units and arrange them to represent an $x^2 + 3x + 2$ rectangle. Students working in base 3 would need:

→

$$x^2 + 3x + 2$$

Figure 4.3

Ask the groups to compare their rectangles and ask them what they notice. Have they found an arrangement that works in all bases?

They should agree that the factors of $x^2 + 3x + 2$ are $(x + 1)$ and $(x + 2)$.

$$x^2 + 3x + 2$$

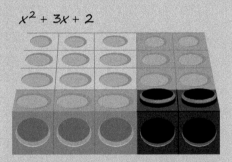

Figure 4.4

You could then ask the groups to make a rectangle using 1 square, 7 sticks and 12 units. Notice that students working in bases 2, 3, 4 and 5 may make arrangements that are not transferable to all other bases. Can they agree on a configuration that works in all bases?

You could also ask the groups to make a rectangle using 1 square, 5 sticks and 8 units. In this case it is possible to make rectangles in bases 2, 3, 4 and 8, but it is not possible to find an arrangement that works in all bases; $x^2 + 5x + 8$ does not factorise.

→

19

Finally, give students time to explore different combinations of squares, sticks and units and ask them to come up with a quick method for deciding whether a combination of squares, sticks and units can be made into a rectangle that works in all bases (that is, Which quadratic polynomials can be factorised?).

Developing independence

Many students struggle to get started on mathematical problems. In some classrooms, a teacher might set the students a challenge, only to see a wave of hands rise up into the air pleading for help. Such students clearly need to develop some independence in their Mathematics classrooms. Often the cause is learnt helplessness, where the students who have received too much help at an earlier age have become reliant on teachers ever since. Your challenge is to provide activities that develop their independence and confidence while ensuring that you also address the curriculum requirements. In Lesson idea 4.2, the use of Multilink cubes enabled students to access an activity involving different bases. Another way to develop independent learning is by using 'low-threshold, high-ceiling' tasks (see Chapter 10 **Inclusive education**) which aim to be accessible to all students and can also provide increasing levels of challenge.

▨ LESSON IDEA ONLINE 4.3: WHAT'S POSSIBLE?

This problem (www.nrich.maths.org/whatspossible) encourages independent learning while addressing a key area of the curriculum, namely expressing numbers as the difference between two square numbers. An accessible starting point is to ask students for a number between 1 and 30 and then record it on the board as the difference between two squares.

For example, if a student offers 27, you could write $27 = 6^2 - 3^2$. →

Repeat the process for some other numbers such as:

$15 = 8^2 - 7^2$ and $4^2 - 1^2$

and $25 = 5^2 - 0^2$

Challenge individuals or pairs to generate further examples for numbers below 30, and encourage them to record their ideas on the board. Students can collaborate and check that they have all the possible solutions for numbers under 30.

Encourage students to reflect on their results and ask them to consider some of the following questions:

1 Is it possible to write every number as the difference between two square numbers?
2 What is special about the numbers that cannot be expressed as the difference between two square numbers?
3 What is special about the difference between the squares of consecutive numbers?
4 What is special about the difference between the squares of numbers that differ by 2? By 3? By 4? ...

Encourage students to share their ideas and present their findings to the rest of the class. This can lead students to generalise and discover the important identity $a^2 - b^2 = (a + b)(a - b)$.

Students could be challenged to represent the identity diagrammatically.

The initial threshold for 'What's Possible?' is very low, building on some simple initial examples, but, as we have seen, this activity can then lead to interesting generalisations and important discoveries.

Teacher Tip

As a plenary activity, give the class a number and challenge them to find all the ways in which it can be written as the difference between two squares, or convince the the rest of the class that it can't be done.

4 Approaches to learning and teaching Mathematics

Summary

Our students may arrive in our Mathematics classroom lacking independent learning skills, displaying a reluctance to use practical resources or failing to appreciate the pleasure that can come from working on mathematical problems. However, we can overcome these obstacles by:

- Modelling the use of resources, we can help students appreciate their power for developing deeper understanding and communicating mathematical ideas.

- Choosing low-threshold, high-ceiling activities we can offer students accessible starting points and suitable follow-up challenges that allow them to work independently at an appropriate level.

- Choosing activities that engage our students, we may find that our students begin to share our enthusiasm for the subject.

Interpreting a syllabus

5

Introduction

A syllabus is a list of requirements that are to be taught on a particular course and usually describes how it is to be examined at the end. It is often set by an exam board or a national body.

Exam boards may use terminology such as subject aims, learning outcomes and assessment objectives. Schools often refer to the syllabus as the subject knowledge and skills that students need in order to satisfy assessment criteria. However, passing an exam is only one part of what we want our students to achieve. We also want them to develop mathematical habits of mind and appreciate the richness of Mathematics. When looking at a syllabus, it is important that we plan schemes of work and units of study that reflect the full range of activities that we consider to be mathematical. This can easily be pushed to one side, particularly when teaching in a 'results-driven' environment. The rest of this chapter will suggest how you can provide a rich mathematical experience for all your students while addressing the requirements of the syllabus.

Weaving the strands of mathematical proficiency

The rope model, proposed in Chapter 4 of '*Adding It Up: Helping Children Learn Mathematics*' (www.nap.edu/read/9822/chapter/6), shows five intertwined strands of mathematical proficiency (Figure 5.1). The authors explain: 'These strands are not independent; they represent different aspects of a complex whole... The five strands are interwoven and interdependent in the development of proficiency in Mathematics. Mathematical proficiency is not a one-dimensional trait, and it cannot be achieved by focusing on just one or two of these strands.' The research behind this model shows that students' proficiency in each individual strand is stronger when we teach in a way that addresses all five strands.

These are the five strands of mathematical proficiency:

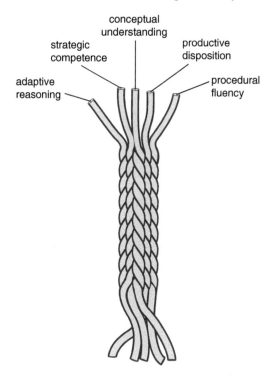

Figure 5.1

Conceptual understanding

Students with conceptual understanding know more than isolated facts and methods. They understand why mathematical ideas are important and can apply them in different contexts. They learn new ideas with understanding, by connecting them to what they already know.

Procedural fluency

Students who are proficient in this strand understand when and how to use procedures, and have the necessary skills to perform them flexibly, accurately and efficiently.

Strategic competence

Strategic competence is required 'to formulate, represent and solve mathematical problems'.

Look at the following strategies to calculate 8×15 (Figure 5.2). Are any of these strategies better or worse than any other?

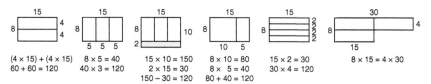

Figure 5.2

Adaptive reasoning

This refers to students' capacity to use logical thought, explanations and justifications. 'In Mathematics, adaptive reasoning is the glue that holds everything together.... In Mathematics, deductive reasoning is used to settle disputes and disagreements.'

Productive disposition

Students with a productive disposition think that Mathematics is useful and worthwhile, believe that with effort and perseverance it can be learnt and applied, and see themselves as capable of making sense of it.

Planning linked activities

Consider the syllabus content statement:

Calculate the mean, median, mode and range for individual and discrete data.

It is tempting to divide this into four lesson objectives, one for each type of average and range, and then address each one separately. Instead, you could plan a series of linked lessons that address all the objectives while developing all aspects of students' mathematical proficiency.

Here are two lesson ideas, based on linked NRICH problems, which address this syllabus content.

LESSON IDEA 5.1: UNEQUAL AVERAGES
(www.nrich.maths.org/11281)

Here's an interesting set of five numbers:

2, 5, 5, 6, 7

The mean, mode, median and range are all 5.

Try to find other sets of five positive whole numbers where:

Mean = Median = Mode = Range

Stop for a moment before reading on. Try the problem yourself. Continue until you can generate sets with ease.

Now think about the following questions:

1 Which of the five strands have you drawn upon?
2 Did you need to be fluent when working out means, modes and medians?
3 Did you use any strategies to find new sets after you'd found the first few?
4 Did you develop any new insights along the way?
5 Did your reasoning and strategies change as you got to know the problem?
6 How does it feel to know that you can find an infinite set of numbers?

Have a look at this possible follow-up task:

Can you find sets of five positive whole numbers that satisfy the following properties?

Mode   <   Median   <   Mean

Mode   <   Mean   <   Median

Mean   <   Mode   <   Median

Mean   <   Median   <   Mode

Median   <   Mode   <   Mean

Median   <   Mean   <   Mode

Again, stop for a moment before reading on and try the problem yourself.

→

Which of the five strands have you drawn upon this time?

Here is a final challenge:

You may have found that not all of the inequalities can be satisfied with sets of five numbers! Can you explain why?

Can you show that all of them can be satisfied with sets of six numbers?

We like this problem because it combines a need for procedural fluency alongside the development of other skills.

'Wipeout' is a task that could follow on from 'Unequal Averages'.

LESSON IDEA 5.2: WIPEOUT
(www.nrich.maths.org/wipeout)

- Take the numbers 1, 2, 3, 4, 5, 6 and choose one to wipe out. For example, you might wipe out 5, leaving you with 1, 2, 3, 4, 6. The mean of what is left is 3.2.

- Is it possible to wipe out one number from 1 to 6, and leave behind an average that is a whole number?

- What about starting with other sets of numbers from 1 to N, where N is even, wiping out just one number and finding the mean?

- Which numbers can be wiped out, so that the mean of what is left is a whole number? Can you explain why?

- What happens when N is odd?

Stop for a moment before reading on and try the problem yourself.

- Would you use this problem with your students?

- Which of the five strands would they require?

More NRICH problems that require students to work with averages can be found at www.nrich.maths.org/averages

---

Teacher Tip

When planning your scheme of work, create a document with each of the subject content statements from the syllabus. Then populate the document with tasks that address the statement and also develop students' mathematical proficiency.

Selecting a sequence of activities

Here is a longer sequence of linked algebraic activities to consider. As you work through the tasks, think about which of the five strands are being developed as the content is being built up during the sequence.

'Perimeter Expressions'

Start with the NRICH problem 'Perimeter Expressions' (www.nrich.maths.org/perimeterexpressions).

Cut a large rectangular piece of paper in half, take one of the halves and cut that in half again. Continue until you have five rectangles. Label the lengths as shown.

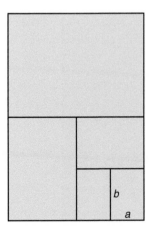

Figure 5.3

Can you combine the largest and smallest rectangles to create a shape with a perimeter of $10a + 4b$?

Can you combine them in a different way to create a shape with a perimeter of $8a + 6b$?

If you create other shapes by combining rectangles so that they meet along an edge with corners touching, what can you say about their perimeters in terms of a and b?

Think about which of the five strands you drew upon before moving on to the next task.

'Always a Multiple'

The NRICH problem 'Always a Multiple' (www.nrich.maths.org/alwaysamultiple) builds on the previous activity by exploring number tricks and asking why they work.

1   Start by thinking of a two-digit number. Reverse the digits and add your answer to your original number. Your answer should be a multiple of 11. Can you explain why?
2   Next take any two-digit number. Add its digits, and subtract your answer from your original number. What do you notice? Can you explain your result?
3   Now try taking any three-digit number. Reverse the digits, and subtract your answer from your original number. What do you notice? Can you explain your result?
4   Can you create a similar number trick of your own?

These first two problems invited you to create algebraic expressions and to simplify them in order to discover and explain your findings. Which of the five strands have come into play so far?

More NRICH problems that require students to create and manipulate algebraic expressions can be found at www.nrich.maths.org/algebraicexpressions

'Pair Products'

At a later stage, you could offer students the NRICH problem 'Pair Products' (www.nrich.maths.org/pairproducts):

1 Choose four consecutive whole numbers.
2 Multiply the first and last numbers together.
3 Multiply the middle pair together.
4 Choose several different sets of four consecutive whole numbers and do the same.
   What do you notice?
5 Can you explain what you have noticed? Will it always happen?
6 Now compare the product of the first and last numbers with the product of the second and penultimate numbers, when you have:

   $5, 6, 7, 8, \ldots x$ consecutive whole numbers
   $4, 5, 6, 7, 8, \ldots x$ consecutive even or odd numbers
   4 consecutive multiples of $3, 4, 5 \ldots$

This problem offers an opportunity to practise the routine algebraic procedure of expanding brackets. Did any of the five strands come into play?

'What's Possible?'

You could follow this activity with the NRICH problem 'What's Possible?' (www.nrich.maths.org/whatspossible):

1 Many numbers can be expressed as the difference of two perfect squares.
   For example: $15 = 4^2 - 1^2$
                    $16 = 5^2 - 3^2$
                    $17 = 9^2 - 8^2$

   Which numbers can you express as the difference of two perfect squares?

2 Can any be expressed as the difference of two perfect squares in more than one way?

These last two problems offer opportunities to generalise and to use algebra for justifications and proof.

Would you use these problems with your students?
Which of the five strands would come into play?

Approaches to learning and teaching Mathematics

More NRICH problems that require students to expand and factorise quadratics can be found at www.nrich.maths.org/expanding

---

Teacher Tip

When you're planning a sequence, try to ensure that all five strands have been addressed. It is worth annotating which strands are being addressed by each task you include in your scheme of work.

Summary

The mathematical proficiency model prepares students to satisfy tightly focussed assessment criteria while also addressing all aspects of their mathematical development.

When planning a series of lessons, ask yourself these questions:

- Will my chosen tasks improve conceptual understanding?

- Will students have a chance to practise standard procedures?

- Will students be required to think strategically?

- Will there be opportunities to develop reasoning skills?

- Will we be encouraging our students to have a productive disposition by:
  - offering them engaging activities?
  - offering them opportunities to be successful?

Active learning

6

What is active learning?

Active learning is a pedagogical practice that places student learning at its centre. It focuses on *how* students learn, not just on *what* they learn. We as teachers need to encourage students to 'think hard', rather than passively receive information. Active learning encourages students to take responsibility for their learning and supports them in becoming independent and confident learners in school and beyond.

Research shows us that it is not possible to transmit understanding to students by simply telling them what they need to know. Instead, we need to make sure that we challenge students' thinking and support them in building their own understanding. Active learning encourages more complex thought processes, such as evaluating, analysing and synthesising, which foster a greater number of neural connections in the brain. While some students may be able to create their own meaning from information received passively, others will not. Active learning enables all students to build knowledge and understanding in response to the opportunities we provide.

Why adopt an active learning approach?

We can enrich all areas of the curriculum, at all stages, by embedding an active learning approach.

In active learning, we need to think not only about the content but also about the process. It gives students greater involvement and control over their learning. This encourages all students to stay focused on their learning, which will often give them greater enthusiasm for their studies. Active learning is intellectually stimulating and taking this approach encourages a level of academic discussion with our students that we, as teachers, can also enjoy. Healthy discussion means that students are engaging with us as a partner in their learning.

Students will better be able to revise for examinations in the sense that revision really is 're-vision' of the ideas that they already understand.

Active learning develops students' analytical skills, supporting them to be better problem solvers and more effective in their application of knowledge. They will be prepared to deal with challenging and unexpected situations. As a result, students are more confident in continuing to learn once they have left school and are better equipped for the transition to higher education and the workplace.

What are the challenges of incorporating active learning?

When people start thinking about putting active learning into practice, they often make the mistake of thinking more about the activity they want to design than about the learning. The most important thing is to put the student and the learning at the centre of our planning. A task can be quite simple but still get the student to think critically and independently. Sometimes a complicated task does not actually help to develop the students' thinking or understanding at all. We need to consider carefully what we want our students to learn or understand and then shape the task to activate this learning.

Introduction

When we visit a new colleague's classroom in their first few weeks as a newly qualified maths teacher, what do we tend to see? All too often, it's a colleague relishing their new role but clearly exhausted by it too. There is frequently an imbalance between the effort that they put into their lessons compared to that of their students. We can explore with them alternative ways to plan their lessons, aiming to ensure that their students put in as much, if not more, effort than they do. We hope that later observations will reveal the emerging success of their new strategies, their students becoming increasingly active participants in their lessons rather than empty vessels to be filled by their teachers' instruction.

In this chapter, we will explore ways in which you can nurture active learners in your Mathematics classrooms. We will consider ways to stimulate students' mathematical curiosity with thought-provoking questions and consider how to draw upon students' learning powers in order to help them develop as independent learners. Crucially, active learning does not diminish the requirement for our students to have a secure knowledge of the curriculum so each of our activities will include purposeful practice of vital mathematical skills.

Mathematical powers

One of the most powerful ways to nurture young mathematicians is to encourage them to use and develop their mathematical powers (Mason, 2007). These powers can be harnessed to move the focus from teachers to students, encouraging students to take more responsibility for their learning. We shall focus on the following powers:

- imagining and expressing
- specialising and generalising
- conjecturing and convincing
- organising and categorising.

Teacher Tip

Before focusing on our students' mathematical powers, it can be incredibly revealing to try to become more aware about how we use our own mathematical powers. Choose a suitable mathematical problem, perhaps one from NRICH's 'Thinking Mathematically' collection (www.nrich.maths.org/mathematically). Have a go at your chosen problem and reflect upon which mathematical powers you draw upon at different stages during the problem-solving process. Do you tend to favour making conjectures early on? Or, are you more focused on organising your work at an early stage? Perhaps you prefer to draw diagrams? Think carefully about how you make use of each of your powers. Reflect on your strongest mathematical powers and how those strengths might influence your classroom teaching. Which of your powers might you want to develop further?

You can develop the mathematical powers of your students in your lessons by recognising and highlighting the different powers required when tackling different problems. Although students might draw upon all their mathematical powers at different points during a lesson, some lessons offer opportunities to develop particular pairs of powers.

Specialising and generalising

Let's start by exploring a circles theorem activity that focuses on the mathematical powers of specialising and generalising.

🖸 LESSON IDEA ONLINE 6.1: CYCLIC QUADRILATERALS

(www.nrich.maths.org/cyclic)

In this activity, students will explore the relationship between opposite angles in cyclic quadrilaterals, building on their knowledge of circles and angles in triangles. This activity begins by focusing on specific cases, allowing students to notice patterns and make conjectures. This initial phase offers students an opportunity to specialise. Then the activity broadens to allow students to make more general conjectures, which lead to generalisations, justifications and proof. The activity offers students an opportunity

→

to discover and prove that the opposite angles in cyclic quadrilaterals add up to 180°.

Throughout this activity, you may initially ask your students to only draw cyclic quadrilaterals that contain the centre of the circle within them.

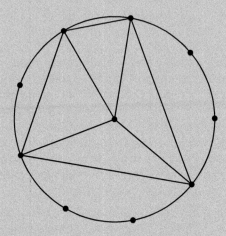

Figure 6.1

Start by drawing a quadrilateral whose vertices lie on the dots of an equally spaced nine-point circle (Figure 6.1). Then draw lines from the centre of the circle to the vertices of the quadrilateral. What do your students notice? What do they know about the angles? The ensuing discussion should draw attention to the isosceles triangles that have been created, and to the possibility of finding the angles of the quadrilateral by first working out the angles of the isosceles triangles.

Allow students time to draw different quadrilaterals on a nine-point circle, and then ask them to calculate their angles by first working out the angles of the isosceles triangles that can be drawn by joining the centre of the circle to each of the vertices. Ask them to record the angles of each quadrilateral in order, working either clockwise or anticlockwise. Collect their results on the board.

Students may have drawn quadrilaterals with the following angles:

Quadrilateral 1: 120°, 80°, 60°, 100°

Quadrilateral 2: 100°, 100°, 80°, 80°

Quadrilateral 3: 140°, 100°, 40°, 80°

Quadrilateral 4: 60°, 60°, 120°, 120°

→

What do they notice about the angles of their cyclic quadrilaterals?

They may notice that the sum of the angles is always 360° (which should not come as a surprise!), that the angles are all multiples of 20°, and most importantly, that the opposite angles add up to 180° (the first and third angles add up to 180°, and so do the second and fourth).

At this point, your students may be tempted to generalise. But can they be sure that the opposite angles of any cyclic quadrilateral will add up to 180°? What would they need to do to convince a sceptic?

Hopefully someone will suggest drawing cyclic quadrilaterals on a circle with a different number of dots. Offer them 10-point, 12-point, 15-point and 18-point circles, and ask them to repeat the previous exercise on a sheet of their choice. All their results should support the conjecture that the opposite angles of all cyclic quadrilaterals add up to 180°. But do they have enough evidence to be sure? What if the dots on the circle are not equally spaced?

Draw a cyclic quadrilateral on the board, with vertices placed randomly along a circle. Then join the centre of the circle to each of the vertices and label the equal angles of the isosceles triangles with identical symbols. Challenge your students to use this diagram to prove that the opposite angles of all cyclic quadrilaterals add up to 180°.

Can they adapt their argument to show that their findings will still hold when the centre of the circle is not within the quadrilateral?

The sum of the angles at opposite vertices of a cyclic quadrilateral is 180 degrees. This is the same for all cyclic quadrilaterals, regardless of the positioning of the centre dot. For example, on a circle with nine points:

In Diagram 1, a (80°) + d (100°) = 180° and b (80°) + c (100°) = 180°.

In Diagram 2 (the centre dot isn't in the quadrilateral) a (60°) + c (120°) = 180° and b (140°) + d (40°) = 180°.

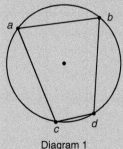

Diagram 1

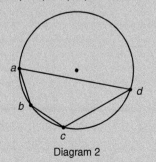

Diagram 2

Figure 6.2

➜

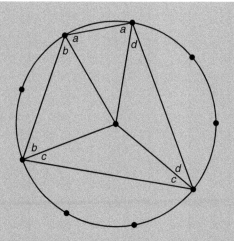

Figure 6.3

'Cyclic Quadrilaterals' is a rich activity for developing students' powers to specialise and generalise. During the activity, students may of course also draw upon their other mathematical powers. They should be encouraged to reflect on which powers they relied upon most, which they used most effectively and which they need to develop further in future activities.

Teacher Tip

Display the mathematical powers prominently in your classroom. Refer to them regularly in lessons so that they become embedded in classroom practice. Encourage students to reflect on which powers they rely on most often, and to identify which powers are under-used and could be developed more fully.

Conjecturing and convincing

In our next activity, students will have another opportunity to make use of their mathematical powers, conjecturing and convincing in particular, and will also work towards discovering another well-known mathematical theorem.

☑ LESSON IDEA ONLINE 6.2: TILTED SQUARES

(www.nrich.maths.org/tiltedsquares)

Most students will be familiar with finding the areas of squares when they are in their usual orientation (Figure 6.4), so we could start by asking 'What is the area of a 4 by 4 square?' and 'How about 5 by 5?', '6 by 6?', '10 by 10?' ...

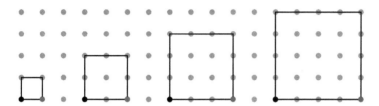

Figure 6.4

Answers should come easily until we ask 'But what if we had to work out the area of a tilted square?' Show students a diagram of a tilted square (Figure 6.5) and ask 'How might we work out the area of this square?'. Allow some thinking time before collecting initial ideas on the board.

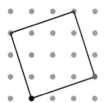

Figure 6.5

Possible feedback might include suggestions that the base is 3 cm long and that the area must therefore be 9 cm². Perhaps a student might suggest measuring the length with a ruler and then squaring the result. John Mason recommends asking students to convince themselves, before convincing their friends, before finally convincing a sceptic, or the rest of the class (2007). This might be a good opportunity to ask students to do this, so that they learn to develop, test and refine their arguments as they go along.

Walk around the classroom and listen to the discussions. Look out for any students who suggest splitting up the square into right-angled triangles and squares and adding the areas, or drawing a 4 by 4 square around the tilted square, then working out the area of the larger square

Approaches to learning and teaching Mathematics

($16\,\text{cm}^2$) and subtracting the area of the four unwanted right-angled triangles ($6\,\text{cm}^2$) to work out the area of the tilted square ($10\,\text{cm}^2$).

Once students have shared their strategies and agreed on the area, mention how good it would be if they could work out the areas of tilted squares as quickly as they calculated the areas of the 'normal' squares.

This is an ideal opportunity for some collaborative work. Suggest that the job of finding the areas of 'slightly tilted' squares could be shared out, and ask different groups to work out the areas of squares with a base that goes 4 along and 1 up, 5 along and 1 up, 6 along and 1 up … 10 along and 1 up …Allow each group time to find the area of their squares before bringing them back together to share their findings. They should notice that all the areas are 1 more than a square number and this should suggest a quick and efficient way to calculate areas of 'slightly tilted' squares.

1 ups

I will start with the basic '1 up' sequence. It goes as follows:

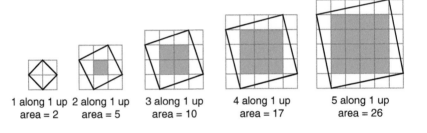

| 1 along 1 up area = 2 | 2 along 1 up area = 5 | 3 along 1 up area = 10 | 4 along 1 up area = 17 | 5 along 1 up area = 26 |

These are some examples of '1 up' titled squares.
I will now draw up a table showing the areas, uses of triangles and squares.

along	up	area of upright square	+	number of triangles	×	area of triangle	=	area of tilted square
1	1	0		4		$\frac{1}{2}$		2
2	1	1		4		1		5
3	1	4		4		$1\frac{1}{2}$		10
4	1	9		4		2		17
5	1	16		4		$2\frac{1}{2}$		26
6	1	25		4		3		37
n	1	$n-1^2$		4		$\frac{1}{2}n$		n (area)

Figure 6.6

In the student's work (Figure 6.6), there is clear evidence of someone using a range of mathematical powers. The student has specialised when drawing different tilted squares, then organised and classified when listing the results in a table, and generalised in the final row of the table.

'Tilted Squares' is an excellent vehicle for introducing Pythagoras' Theorem. Rather than presenting the theorem as a fait accompli, students can discover the relationship between the squares of the sides of right-angled triangles by generalising their findings. But can they prove their results?

Sketch the tilted square within a square shown in Figure 6.7.

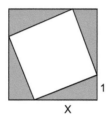

Figure 6.7

Ask students whether they can work out the area of the tilted square using the 'boxing in' method described earlier.

By subtracting the area of the four shaded triangles from the area of the larger square, they can arrive at the area of the tilted square:

Area of larger square − area of four shaded triangles $= (x + 1)^2 - 4(\frac{1}{2} x)$

$$= x^2 + 2x + 1 - 2x$$

$$= x^2 + 1^2$$

Encourage your students to next consider squares with different tilts, such as 2, 3, 4 or 5 up. This may again offer an opportunity for collaborative work, with different groups taking on squares of different tilts, working out their areas and trying to generalise their results.

Figure 6.8 is an example of how a student recorded her results after working on three steps up and four steps up tilted squares.

Let's look at the pattern for the area of '3 ups'

x	1	2	3	4	5	6	x
area	10	13	18	25	34	45	$x^2 + 9$

Let's see '4 ups'

x	1	2	3	4	5	6	x
area	17	20	25	34	45	58	$x^2 + 16$

This proves that to be an area of a tilted square the number must be the sum of two square numbers.

$$x^2 + n^2 = \text{area of tilted square}$$

If you were also only given the number along and the number up you could find the area because: number along^2 + number up^2 = area. This can be proved by Pythagoras' Theorem.

Figure 6.8

She appears to have convinced herself that her results prove Pythagoras' Theorem, but we may require a more rigorous justification …

Draw a tilted square with an x along, y up tilt, and ask your students whether they can work out the area of this general tilted square. Again, the 'boxing-in' method can be used:

$$\text{Area of larger square} - \text{area of four shaded triangles} = (x + y)^2 - 2xy$$
$$= x^2 + 2xy + y^2 - 2xy$$
$$= x^2 + y^2$$

Students will now have discovered and proved Pythagoras' Theorem!

Teacher Tip

By encouraging a whole class to work on a problem together, giving students responsibility for working on different aspects and then sharing their results, students begin to appreciate the benefit of belonging to a 'community of mathematicians'.

A vision for Mathematics teaching

Before we consider our next activity, we should perhaps reflect on Dave Hewitt's concerns that mathematical exploration can be interpreted too narrowly in some classrooms (Hewitt, 1992). He has argued that mathematical problem-solving can become formulaic if it simply requires teachers to introduce an investigation, allow time for their students to record their findings in a table, notice a pattern and then complete the exercise by producing a generalised algebraic statement (www.nrich.maths.org/trainspotters). In our first two examples of active learning, students have had an opportunity to rehearse how to work out angles and areas, and have needed to go beyond pattern-spotting, by not only testing conjectures and making generalisations, but also by proving important mathematical results.

Purposeful practice

In our third example, we will move our focus towards an active learning activity that offers opportunities for the purposeful practice of prior knowledge and skills in calculating surface areas.

☑ LESSON IDEA ONLINE 6.3: CUBOIDS
(www.nrich.maths.org/cuboidchallenge)

You could start by sharing students' different approaches for finding the surface area of cuboids and discussing which approach they consider to be most efficient. Having plenty of cuboids in the classroom, such as cereal boxes, can provide visual aids for your students to explain their ideas to each other.

When you are satisfied that your students can calculate the surface area of a cuboid, set them the main challenge. Can they find the dimensions of a cuboid that has a surface area of exactly 100 square units? If your students have become accustomed to using and recognising their mathematical powers, you could also encourage them to predict which mathematical powers they expect to use during this task.

They may already realise that the task will require them to work systematically by organising and categorising their ideas. Encourage them to keep a record of what they tried that didn't work, as well as what did work. It can be helpful for them to share their ideas, including ones that don't work, on the class board. In this initial working session, try to ensure that students are calculating surface area correctly.

6

Approaches to learning and teaching Mathematics

Sometimes problem-solving can seem a daunting task. To help students realise the progress that they are making, it can be helpful to draw a ladder on the board where each step up represents a step forward in the problem-solving process:

- I'll change the question to ...
- why I'm sure I have all the solutions
- all solutions
- some solutions
- one solution
- no solutions yet
- calculations going wrong.

If students are struggling to get started, a useful strategy is to simplify the problem. In this case, you could encourage students to initially focus on cuboids where all of the lengths are equal, and check whether any of them satisfy the requirement for a surface area of $100\,cm^2$.

If some students are moving up the ladder more slowly than others, then a short group discussion could suggest strategies for working systematically that might help students move up the ladder more quickly. Some students may choose to fix the width and the height, and just adjust the length of the cuboids, and check to see whether any combination leads to the required surface area.

Challenge students who reach the top of the ladder quickly to identify which surface areas under $100\,cm^2$ have the greatest number of cuboids, and why.

Allocate some time at the end of the lesson to reflect on what your students have achieved, which methods and ideas were most useful and which aspects of the problem remain unanswered. They could also reflect upon which mathematical powers they relied on during the challenge and compare their ideas to those they offered before they started the problem. The subject of cuboids combines an active learning task with the purposeful practice of key mathematical skills.

Summary

- Some of the best active learning lessons begin by posing a question that taps into students' natural curiosity.

- Active learning lessons are often more memorable and engaging, and usually demand that our students work harder than in more traditional lessons.

- The most successful active learning lessons often encourage students to draw upon their range of mathematical powers. We need to encourage our students to recognise and reflect on their different powers, especially how they use them and which they need to develop further.

- Active learning does not preclude rehearsing important skills. By choosing activities carefully, we can provide active lessons that also develop fluency in key skills.

7

Assessment for Learning

What is Assessment for Learning?

Assessment for Learning (AfL) is a teaching approach that generates feedback that can be used to improve students' performance. Students become more involved in the learning process and, from this, gain confidence in what they are expected to learn and to what standard. We as teachers gain insights into a student's level of understanding of a particular concept or topic, which helps to inform how we support their progression.

We need to understand the meaning and method of giving purposeful feedback to optimise learning. Feedback can be informal, such as oral comments to help students think through problems, or formal, such as the use of rubrics to help clarify and scaffold learning and assessment objectives.

Why use Assessment for Learning?

By following well-designed approaches to AfL, we can understand better how our students are learning and use this to plan what we will do next with a class or individual students (see Figure 7.1). We can help our students to see what they are aiming for and to understand what they need to do to get there. AfL makes learning visible; it helps students understand more accurately the nature of the material they are learning and themselves as learners. The quality of interactions and feedback between students and teachers becomes critical to the learning process.

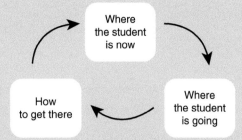

Figure 7.1: How can we use this plan to help our students?

We can use AfL to help our students focus on specific elements of their learning and to take greater responsibility for how they might move forward. AfL creates a valuable connection between assessment and learning activities, as the clarification of objectives will have a direct impact on how we devise teaching and learning strategies. AfL techniques can support students in becoming more confident in what they are learning, reflective in how they are learning, more likely to try out new approaches, and more engaged in what they are being asked to learn.

What are the challenges of incorporating AfL?

The use of AfL does not mean that we need to test students more frequently. It would be easy to just increase the amount of summative assessment and use this formatively as a regular method of helping us decide what to do next in our teaching. We can judge how much learning has taken place through ways other than testing, including, above all, communicating with our students in a variety of ways and getting to know them better as individuals.

Introduction

In a Mathematics classroom, there are many ways in which we can effectively use assessment to promote learning and inform our planning. If we choose tasks carefully and encourage discussion that reveals our students' thinking, we can gain insight into what they understand, from the very beginning of a topic right through to the final assessment. If we do not know what is going on in our students' heads, it is much more difficult to plan and teach effectively! Good Mathematics is not done in isolation, so this chapter also looks at how to promote self- and peer-assessment.

Using tasks to find out what students know

There are many ways of finding out what students already know at the start of a topic. We can set a pre-test, have a class brainstorming session, or invite students to respond to questions with mini whiteboards, or number fans. These methods give us some sense of what students can do, but it's not always easy to address what they can't do, particularly if different students are struggling with different aspects of the content. One way to overcome this challenge is to set a task that can elicit what students know and understand, but also has some mathematically interesting features that make it engaging, even for students who are already comfortable with the content.

☑ **LESSON IDEA ONLINE 7.1: FACTORS AND MULTIPLES PUZZLE**

This NRICH puzzle (www.nrich.maths.org/factorpuzzle) invites students to place number properties and numbers into a two-way grid (Figure 7.2). As well as needing to understand definitions, students also need to think strategically, because there are some headings that are mutually exclusive. For example, there are no square numbers that are also prime. →

PRIME NUMBERS	3	2	5	7	
FACTORS OF 60	10	12			
NUMBERS LESS THAN 20	6	4		9	
	1				
	TRIANGULAR NUMBERS	EVEN NUMBERS			

SQUARE NUMBERS	
	MULTIPLES OF 3
NUMBERS MORE THAN 20	MULTIPLES OF 5
ODD NUMBERS	

11	15	16	18	20
21	23	24	25	30
35	36	45	55	60

Figure 7.2

All students should be able to make progress straight away, as some of the headings are very straightforward. This means that you can let students get started on the task in pairs without needing to intervene for the first few minutes.

Teacher Tip

You can use this time to circulate and listen in on students' conversations, and start to assess what knowledge is secure and what misconceptions are cropping up. As you overhear what students are saying, collect the questions that have arisen and write them on the board.

Here are some examples of the sort of questions that might arise:

1 Is 1 a prime number?
2 What's a triangular number and how do I work these out?
3 Are there any triangular numbers that are square?
4 Which numbers are both prime and square? Prime and triangular? Even and prime?

→

Then bring the class together: 'Here are some questions that some of you have been discussing. In your pairs, see which of these you think you can answer, and be ready to share your thoughts and reasoning.' Once students have talked with their partner and shared their answers and reasoning, give them a chance to complete the task. This task has several possible solutions (www.nrich.maths.org/factorpuzzle/solution), so students who manage to complete the grid can display their answers on a poster, and then look at what others did differently.

Tasks like this one provide an opportunity to assess skills as well as knowledge. In cases like this, it is useful to tell students explicitly that success is not just about completing the challenge but also about communicating their thoughts clearly, responding to other people's ideas and persevering when they find it hard.

Another way to find out what students know is to present them with a set of mathematical statements and ask them to decide whether each is 'Always', 'Sometimes' or 'Never' true. Here are some suggestions from a variety of different topics:

- Multiples of 4 can be written as the difference of two squares.
- For a set of 5 positive whole numbers, mean < median < mode.
- Quadrilaterals have at least 1 line of symmetry.
- Octagons have fewer than 5 right angles.
- $5n + 2$ is bigger than $3n - 1$.
- In a school, there will be two people who share a birthday.

Teacher Tip

You could collect together a dozen statements for a particular topic and then invite students to sort them into 'Always', 'Sometimes' and 'Never', explaining their reasoning for each.

If they don't know how to get started, suggest that they try some examples such as:

- Can you find an example where it's true?
- Can you find an example where it's not true?

As with the 'Factors and Multiples Puzzle', listen in on students' discussions and write up on the board any statements where there is disagreement.

An interesting extension is to ask students to modify statements that are sometimes true to make them always or never true.

Even if students appear to have a good grasp of a topic, asking them to justify their claims can reveal gaps in their knowledge and understanding.

Whatever task you choose, the value comes from listening to students' discussions. If there are a few minor misunderstandings (for example whether or not 1 is a prime number), these can be dealt with quickly. However, if you notice repeated errors or more serious misconceptions, you can plan future activities to address them.

Developing an AfL classroom

One barrier to effective informal assessment is students' reluctance to speak out when they are unsure or confused. Successful AfL happens in classrooms where students feel comfortable sharing their initial thoughts, the processes that they may be in the middle of, and strategies that don't work. In some classrooms, the only voices you hear are the teacher and the most confident students. In an AfL classroom you might hear the following:

- I think you could start by …
- I tried doing … but it didn't work …
- I got 37 but I'm not sure if it's right.
- Can someone explain how to …
- Is this the best way to …
- I've got this far but I'm not sure what to do next …

The classroom culture recognises that learning is the process of moving from uncertainty to understanding, and that students are not expected to pick up new ideas instantly. This requires students to be sensitive to the needs of the community so that wrong or partial answers are never met with ridicule or impatience. This is why some teachers adopt a 'No hands up' policy where students are chosen at random to answer questions. This ensures that it is not just students who know the answers who do the talking in the class. (See Chapter 9 **Language awareness** for more on 'No hands up'.)

A strategy you can use to encourage all students to contribute is increasing wait time. When asking questions, teachers often give students very little thinking time. When answers aren't instantly forthcoming, there is a temptation to jump in and rephrase the question, answer it yourself, or move on to another student. If you increase wait time to 5 or 10 seconds, you show that you value a thoughtful response. Another strategy is to give students time to think on their own, then time to discuss with a partner before sharing with the class. See Chapter 9 **Language awareness** for a closer look at this strategy.

These two strategies allow us to ask mathematically interesting questions that require students to think a little more deeply, rather than just playing 'Guess what's in the teacher's head'. For example:

- 'Is 1089 a multiple of 3?' could become 'Tell me some numbers between 1000 and 1100 that are multiples of 3.'

- 'What is $\frac{1}{2} - \frac{1}{3}$' could become 'Tell me some fractions between $\frac{1}{3}$ and $\frac{1}{2}$'.

- 'What is the mean of 2, 4 and 9' could become 'Give me a set of 3 numbers whose mean is 5'.

If you want to create a culture of productive discussion and thoughtful reasoning, you must ensure that correct answers are challenged as well as incorrect ones. Ask questions such as 'How do you know?' and 'Why is that true?', to check the depth of students' understanding. It is worth practising a neutral face so you don't accidentally give away whether an answer is right or wrong.

Self-assessment

When students are working on questions alone, there is a risk that they may make the same mistakes over and over again, as you cannot watch 30 students at once to check what they are doing. If instead you choose a task that requires students to collaborate and justify their ideas, they have opportunities to spot their own and each other's mistakes and gaps in understanding. Students are able to assess their own understanding as they test out ideas, and can take responsibility for their own learning. This frees you up to intervene when students are unable to resolve a difficulty for themselves.

☑ LESSON IDEA ONLINE 7.2: ISOSCELES TRIANGLES

Here is an extract from the NRICH problem 'Isosceles Triangles' (www.nrich.maths.org/isosceles). This question is about isosceles triangles with an area of $9\,cm^2$.

Each vertex of the triangle must be at a grid point of a square grid, so all the vertices will have whole-number coordinates.

One of the vertices must be at the point (20, 20).

How many different triangles satisfy these four conditions?

Ask students to work in group. Students working alone might find half a dozen examples, think they have found all the possibilities, and say that they have finished. Alternatively, they might find some incorrect examples and not notice that they have made a mistake. Instead, students working in groups can check each other's work for mistakes and omissions, and they can rehearse with each other their justification that they haven't missed any possibilities.

Encourage students to speak up if they disagree with or don't understand another student. Make it clear that you expect a final answer that is agreed on and understood by everyone in the group.

Teacher Tip

One strategy is to let groups know that you will be choosing a member at random to report back to the whole class, so it is their responsibility to ensure that everyone in the group is prepared to share their group's thinking.

By starting a topic with a group task to assess what students already know, you can then plan in a way that responds to their needs. If they find the task straightforward, you can offer challenging extensions. If they find it more difficult than anticipated, you can spend more time on the basics. This responsive approach to planning lies at the very heart of AfL.

☑ LESSON IDEA ONLINE 7.3: PAINTED CUBE

Take a look at the NRICH task 'Painted Cube'
(www.nrich.maths.org/paintedcube):

1 Imagine a large cube made up from 27 small red cubes.

2 Imagine dipping the large cube into a pot of yellow paint so
  that the whole outer surface is covered, and then breaking the
  cube up into its small cubes.

3 How many of the small cubes will have yellow paint on their
  faces?

4 Will they all look the same?

As students work in groups on the problem, you may observe
that they find it straightforward to visualise in three dimensions,
in which case you might choose to explore the generalisation
to $n \times n \times n$ cubes. However, if in the first lesson you notice that
they are not confident at working with three-dimensional shapes
and surface area, you could provide cubes and work on some
visualisation activities.

After your students have worked on 'Painted Cube', you will have a
clearer idea of whether they are ready for a new challenge or need time
to consolidate their understanding. On the NRICH website, there are
a selection of problems about volume and surface area that you could
choose from. Here are a few you might like to look at:

- 'Cuboid Challenge' (www.nrich.maths.org/cuboidchallenge)
- 'Partly Painted Cube' (www.nrich.maths.org/partlypainted)
- 'Marbles in a Box' (www.nrich.maths.org/marbles)

By regularly giving students opportunities to work in groups, you offer
them the chance to assess their own understanding and value different
points of view. Students who regularly work collaboratively are more
confident at speaking up, and know when and how to seek help. They
are given a chance to take control of their own learning – a teacher's job
is ultimately to make themselves redundant!

Peer assessment – making good use of student work

So far, we have looked at informal assessment that goes on while students are working. The way we assess students' finished work can have a huge impact on how they learn, so this section explores some of the ways in which student work can be used to promote further learning.

It is important to make the distinction between answers and solutions. An answer is a brief response to the question posed, whereas a solution includes the solver's ideas, why they chose a certain method, and explanations of what they did and what they noticed. A solution tells a story about the process of solving a problem, and gives insight into the problem that an answer alone does not. For students to learn, they need to focus on producing solutions, not just answers. Once your students are in the habit of producing solutions, you can use their work in a variety of ways to support further learning.

☑ LESSON IDEA ONLINE 7.4: WHAT'S IT WORTH?

This NRICH problem (www.nrich.maths.org/whatsitworth) is a great task for helping students to see the difference between an answer and a solution. Take a look at the grid in Figure 7.3. Can you find the missing total that should go where the question mark has been put?

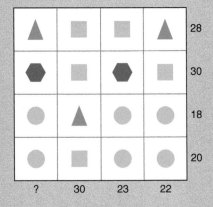

Figure 7.3 →

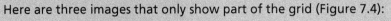

Here are three images that only show part of the grid (Figure 7.4):

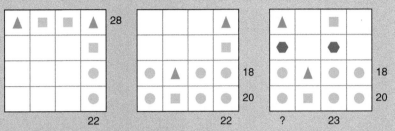

Figure 7.4

From each image, it is possible to make deductions that can lead to the solution. You could give different images to different groups of students, and ask them to see whether they can use the starting point to get to the solution. Then, invite them to present their solution to the rest of the class, and finally spend some time discussing the merits of the various methods. Which did they find easy to understand? Which method was the most elegant? Which method would they use if they had to solve a similar problem? This discussion cements the idea that solutions are valuable and have a purpose, whereas '21', the answer to the question, can quickly be forgotten.

Once students appreciate the difference between answers and solutions, we can start using their finished work to promote further thinking. Here is one model for using student work in the classroom. Start by introducing a problem and give students some time to engage with it independently. After a while, hand out a selection of full or partial solutions. For students who think they have solved the initial problem, these may provoke them to think about refining their strategy and improving their approach. For students who had not solved the problem, seeing other students' work can give them a 'nudge' in the right direction. To use this approach, you need examples of student work.

Teacher Tip

To start off with, it can be useful to use anonymous work from other classes so that students can practise constructive criticism without personalities or class hierarchy getting in the way.

☑ LESSON IDEA ONLINE 7.5: STEEL CABLES

In the NRICH task 'Steel Cables' (www.nrich.maths.org/steelcables), students are given an image of a size 5 cable and challenged to work out the number of strands in a size 10 cable (see Figure 7.5):

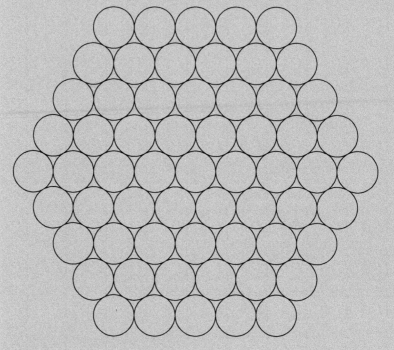

Figure 7.5

In addition, there are four examples of student work that can be shared with the class, together with these questions:

Which approach makes the most sense to you?

What do you like about your favourite approach?

This tactic of sharing multiple solutions challenges those students who like to stick to familiar ways of working. You are making our focus the evaluation of different solutions rather than just aiming to get an answer. You are encouraging students to think more deeply about the Mathematics and giving them opportunities to make connections between different topics.

Once students are confident at evaluating solutions, you can embed self-assessment and peer-assessment in every lesson. Give students time to reflect on what they have produced, and invite them regularly to look at each other's written work and offer constructive feedback. Make sure that they also have opportunities to develop the skill of talking about Mathematics.

Teacher Tip

One way to do this is to invite students out to the board to present their solution to a problem and answer questions from the class. The teacher's role is then to ensure that the classroom culture remains one where students feel safe and value the criticism they receive.

Summary

- At the start of a topic, offer low-threshold high-ceiling tasks to assess where students are in their thinking, pick up misconceptions, and inform the planning of follow-up lessons.

- Group work can be effective in allowing students to verbalise their thinking and refine their ideas while you look for evidence of learning.

- Working collaboratively allows students to assess their own and each other's thinking, so they only need teacher input when they cannot resolve an issue for themselves.

- Student work is not just a finished product but a useful teaching tool.

8 | Metacognition

What is metacognition?

Metacognition describes the processes involved when students plan, monitor, evaluate and make changes to their own learning behaviours. These processes help students to think about their own learning more explicitly and ensure that they are able to meet a learning goal that they have identified themselves or that we, as teachers, have set.

Metacognitive learners recognise what they find easy or difficult. They understand the demands of a particular learning task and are able to identify different approaches they could use to tackle a problem. Metacognitive learners are also able to make adjustments to their learning as they monitor their progress towards a particular learning goal.

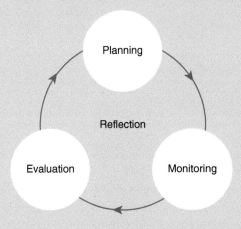

Figure 8.1: A helpful way to think about the phases involved in metacognition.

During the *planning* phase, students think about the explicit learning goal we have set and what we are asking them to do. As teachers, we need to make clear to students what success looks like in any given task before they embark on it. Students build on their prior knowledge, reflect on strategies they have used before and consider how they will approach the new task.

As students put their plan into action, they are constantly *monitoring* the progress they are making towards their learning goal. If the strategies they had decided to use are not working, they may decide to try something different.

Once they have completed the task, students determine how successful the strategy they used was in helping them to achieve their learning goal. During this *evaluation* phase, students think about what went well and what didn't go as well to help them decide what they could do differently next time. They may also think about what other types of problems they could solve using the same strategy.

Reflection is a fundamental part of the plan–monitor–evaluate process and there are various ways in which we can support our students to reflect on their learning process. In order to apply a metacognitive approach, students need access to a set of strategies that they can use and a classroom environment that encourages them to explore and develop their metacognitive skills.

Why teach metacognitive skills?

Research evidence suggests that the use of metacognitive skills plays an important role in successful learning. Metacognitive practices help students to monitor their own progress and take control of their learning. Metacognitive learners think about and learn from their mistakes and modify their learning strategies accordingly. Students who use metacognitive techniques find it improves their academic achievement across subjects, as it helps them transfer what they have learnt from one context to another context, or from a previous task to a new task.

What are the challenges of developing students' metacognitive skills?

For metacognition to be commonplace in the classroom, we need to encourage students to take time to think about and learn from their mistakes. Many students are afraid to make mistakes, meaning that they are less likely to take risks, explore new ways of thinking or tackle unfamiliar problems. We as teachers are instrumental in shaping the culture of learning in a classroom. For metacognitive practices to thrive, students need to feel confident enough to make mistakes, to discuss their mistakes and ultimately to view them as valuable, and often necessary, learning opportunities.

Introduction

If we want our students to develop good metacognitive strategies, we need to help them become aware of what it means to think and work like mathematicians. As discussed in Chapter 3 **The nature of Mathematics**, Mathematics is a unique discipline within the school curriculum, and we should be offering our students a flavour of what's special about the subject. If Mathematics is a way of thinking about the world, then metacognition is a way to become better at doing Mathematics!

Metacognition means being aware of our thought processes, and in Mathematics classrooms, the following thought processes (or 'Habits of Mind') are of key importance:

- 'Being Curious'
- 'Being Thoughtful'
- 'Being Determined'
- 'Being Collaborative'

In this chapter, we will look at the first three; 'Being Collaborative' is covered in detail in other chapters.

Curiosity – theory-building and problem-solving

Fields Medallist Tim Gowers wrote an article a few years ago, describing two aspects of curiosity exhibited by professional mathematicians – theory-building and problem-solving. Roughly speaking, theory-builders try to solve problems in order to understand Mathematics better, and problem-solvers try to understand new mathematics in order to become better at solving problems.

How does this translate to school Mathematics? We think we should be offering our students activities that give them the experience of theory-building and of problem-solving, so that they leave our classrooms with some sense of what it means to be a mathematician.

☑ LESSON IDEA ONLINE 8.1: SUMMING CONSECUTIVE NUMBERS

Consider the problem 'Summing Consecutive Numbers' (www.nrich.maths.org/summingconsecutive). You could start the lesson by asking students to give you a number and then write this on the board expressed as a sum of consecutive positive whole numbers:

'14' 'That's interesting, I can write 14 as 2 + 3 + 4 + 5.'

'21' 'That's also an interesting number, it's 10 + 11 or 6 + 7 + 8'
'45' 'That's very interesting, I can write it as 22 + 23, or 14 + 15 + 16, or 7 + 8 + 9 + 10 + 11 ...'

'8' '... Oh, I don't think I can write this one like the others ...'

Stop for a moment before reading on. What questions are you curious to explore?

At this point, there are several ways to proceed. One strategy is to say to students: 'At the end of the lesson, I'm going to give you a number and I want you to be able to tell me straight away how it can be written as the sum of consecutive numbers.' Alternatively, you could invite students to come up with a list of interesting questions and conjectures that they would like to think about. Either way, we are tapping into students' natural curiosity, and giving them a chance to engage in some theory-building. Students have the chance to develop their understanding of the structure of numbers, and to appreciate the power of algebra for explaining patterns they discover.

Teacher Tip

You might instead choose to use the task to appeal to students with a problem-solving mentality, by posing questions such as 'Which numbers can be written as the sum of three consecutive numbers?' and 'Which numbers cannot be written as consecutive sums?' Although they are closed questions with one right answer, there is a lot to explore along the way. For someone who is motivated by the challenge of problem-solving for its own sake, posing the question this way offers a hook, and new understanding can follow.

The importance of asking good questions

Being a good mathematician is not just about being able to answer questions but also about being able to ask questions. As teachers, we need to think very carefully about the questions we choose to ask and the mathematical behaviours that we are modelling. Here are some prompts you might offer in a lesson. For each one, ask yourself – why might I set this task? What thinking might each task require from my students?

'What is the factorised form of $x^2 + 7x + 6$?'

'Explore quadratics where the coefficient of x is one more than the constant term. Can you describe a way to factorise them?' (See the problem 'Factorising with Multilink' in Chapter 4 **Key considerations** for suggestions on how you might follow this up.)

'Construct a triangle with sides of 4 cm, 5 cm and 6 cm.'

'Generate three random numbers and then construct a triangle with those side lengths. How can you check whether it is possible to draw the triangle?'

Teacher Tip

When you ask questions, think about whether you are giving students an opportunity to be curious, and whether your questions could lead to generalisations. If students find themselves in an environment where challenging and thought-provoking mathematical questions are the norm, they are more likely to become curious mathematicians who pose good questions for themselves.

Thoughtful problem-solvers

In 1945, the Hungarian mathematician George Polya wrote a book called *How to Solve It*, reflecting on what he did to help his students become better problem solvers. He described a 'heuristic', or recipe, for mathematical problem-solving focusing on the metacognitive skills that need to be employed at each stage. Like the planning, monitoring and evaluation phases of the model discussed at the start of this chapter, Polya describes distinct phases of the mathematical problem-solving process:

• Understand the problem.
• Make a plan.
• Carry out the plan.
• Look back.

If we want our students to become confident, capable and reflective problem-solvers, we need to make these steps explicit to them and help them to get into the habit of using this 'recipe' whenever they are faced with a new mathematical challenge.

Quite often, in classrooms, students don't need to work very hard to understand problems, as teachers explain very clearly what they are expected to do. Here are some questions that you might want them to ask themselves when solving problems outside the classroom or in an exam:

• Can I put the problem into my own words?
• What area(s) of Mathematics does this involve?
• What do I know?
• What do I need to know?

Once students understand the problem, Polya says they should plan ahead before getting stuck in, because it might save time later. Encourage your students to ask questions like these:

- Have I seen a problem like this before?
- How could I represent the problem? Numerically? Algebraically? Diagramatically?

Carrying out a plan is straightforward until you get stuck, or uncertain about what to do next. Many students don't realise that, actually, being stuck is a mathematician's default state! Most professional mathematicians spend much of their time thinking, but students often feel uncomfortable if they can't see an answer straightaway. This is exacerbated because students are used to working on exercises by applying a method where they can write the answer straight down without having to think very deeply. Then, when faced with a non-routine problem, they become anxious when they don't know how to proceed.

Stop for a moment and think – 'What strategies do I use when I am stuck? What questions do I ask myself to get unstuck?' You could choose a problem from NRICH's 'Thinking Mathematically' collection, and monitor what you do at each stage of the problem-solving process.

Teacher Tip

Share with your students these questions that they could ask themselves when they are unsure what to do next:

- Is there a special case or a simpler version of the problem that I could try first?
- Could I try some numbers and look for a pattern?
- Can I work backwards?
- Am I working systematically?

The problem '1 Step 2 Step' (https://nrich.maths.org/1step2step) asks students to imagine walking down a staircase with 12 steps, taking 1 or 2 steps at a time. In how many different ways can they go down the steps? This is a great example of a task where the initial problem is just too big to handle, so the best strategy is to try some smaller cases, look for a pattern, explain the pattern and then solve the original problem.

Working systematically is such an important tool in the mathematician's problem-solving kit that we are going to take a closer look at it. Have a look at the NRICH problem 'Two and Two' (www.nrich.maths.org/twoandtwo), a cryptarithm in which each letter represents a different digit (see Figure 8.1):

$$\begin{array}{r} \text{TWO} \\ + \text{TWO} \\ \hline \text{FOUR} \\ \hline \end{array}$$

Figure 8.1

Can you find all the possible solutions? How will you know that you have found them all?

In order to answer questions like this, students will have to organise their work to justify that they have not missed any possibilities. They can learn to work systematically by being challenged to work on problems of this sort on a regular basis. This prepares them for meeting important mathematical concepts such as 'proof by exhaustion'.

As well as working systematically, it's important for students to think strategically. Strategic thinking is all about looking for efficient or elegant methods. We can choose tasks that will help students to appreciate the importance of strategic thinking, and get them used to developing strategies of their own.

☑ LESSON IDEA ONLINE 8.2: WARMSNUG DOUBLE GLAZING

Let's consider strategic thinking in the context of the NRICH problem 'Warmsnug Double Glazing' (www.nrich.maths.org/warmsnug). Look at Figure 8.2. Each window has a price, but one has been priced incorrectly – can you work out which one?

→

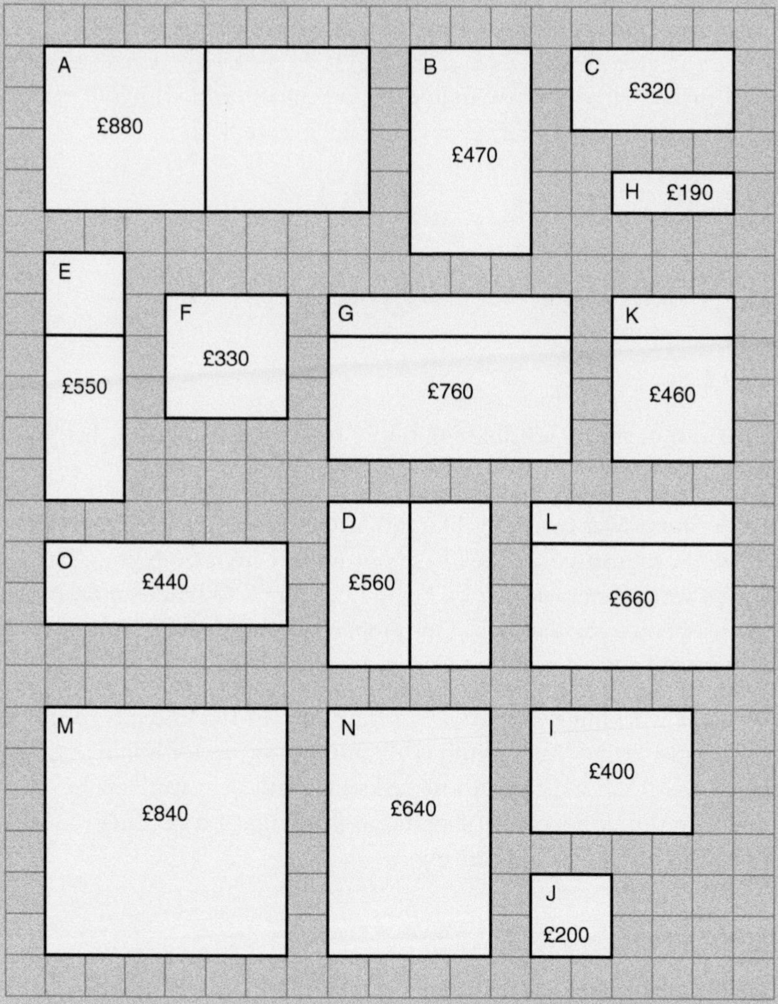

Approaches to learning and teaching Mathematics

Figure 8.2

Start by giving the students the task without any scaffolding. Some may start to compare areas and frame lengths to make deductions, but they may not have a particularly systematic way of working and may not know how to develop a good strategy.

After they have had a chance to think about the problem, offer them the starting points, which could lead them to the solution much faster. Invite them to turn each starting point into a complete solution.

→

- Compare windows K and I because they use the same area of glass.
- Compare windows B and O because they use the same length of frame.
- Compare the cost of buying two of window J with the cost of window B.
- Compare the cost of buying windows C and J with the cost of window K.
- Compare the costs of windows E and O.

Then invite students to discuss which strategy they found most effective and why.

This technique of examining someone else's strategy helps students to develop the 'Looking Back' phase of Polya's problem-solving model – if they are used to critiquing other people's solutions, they will develop the habit of critiquing their own. Looking back is important, because reflection helps us to notice what we did to be successful, which may help us next time we are faced with a similar situation.

Teacher Tip

Encourage students to ask themselves the following questions whenever they finish a problem:

- Have I actually answered the original question?
- Does my answer make sense? Is it consistent?
- Have I solved the problem fully, or is there still more to do?
- What could I have done differently?

Students are very used to seeing neat and tidy mathematics laid out in textbooks, or to seeing the teacher solving a problem on the board that they have rehearsed beforehand. This gives many students the message that to be a good mathematician you have to be able to write down organised ideas without mistakes. Wouldn't it be nice for students, just once in their school life, to see a brave teacher who is prepared to tackle an unfamiliar problem in front of the class? The teacher could articulate their thoughts as they go along, correcting themselves as they make inevitable mistakes, and reflecting on their route to the solution at the end.

For another task to help students develop a strategic and systematic way of working, take a look at 'Reflecting Squarely', (www.nrich.maths.org/reflectingsquarely). Students are invited to find all the possible ways of arranging a set of shapes to create a shape with reflectional symmetry. Once they have worked on the problem, show them the published solution (http://nrich.maths.org/1840/solution) and discuss the elegance of the strategy used.

Fostering determination

Turning 'I can't do it' into 'I can't do it … yet'

It's sometimes hard to understand why students are anxious about Mathematics, especially if it is something we ourselves find straightforward. Yet anxiety about Mathematics can strike us at any time – most of us will at some point have panicked when faced with a problem we did not know how to solve. The first step in dealing with anxiety in our classrooms is acknowledging that it exists.

Once you are aware that some students in your classes feel a fear about Mathematics that perhaps they do not feel about other subjects, you can start to develop a classroom culture that addresses that fear. It helps to acknowledge that some aspects of Mathematics are hard! If students are getting everything right with ease, the chances are that they are not learning very much, and they will find it much more difficult to cope when they finally do meet an obstacle. We believe that every student should be given opportunities to succeed, but equally, every student needs to experience what it is like to struggle. Success feels so much sweeter when it comes after real effort.

Teacher Tip

Share the story of how WD40 got its name. Apparently, Norman Larsen didn't think WD1, 2, 3 … 39 were good enough, but on his 40th attempt he produced the winning formula that is now a household name. Sharing stories like this with your students can help them to realise that the success stories they see in the world around them are usually the result of a long and bumpy process.

Carol Dweck's research has shown that students who have a 'growth mindset' do better than students who have a 'fixed mindset'. If students believe that their capabilities in mathematics are fixed and inherent, there is a good chance that when the going gets tough, they will think they have reached the limit of what they can achieve, and they are more likely to give up. Students who believe that they are capable of growing and making progress will persevere even when they are finding something difficult. As the saying goes, 'Whether you think you can, or whether you think you can't, you are probably right!'

The NRICH problem 'Nine Colours' is a good problem to foster resilience! Take 27 small cubes, 3 each of 9 different colours. Can you arrange them into a $3 \times 3 \times 3$ cube so that each colour appears once on every face? This is a great challenge to set students, because there is no mathematical barrier to entry, but it is very unlikely that anyone will solve it immediately. Students will need to explore, make decisions, consider, backtrack, try again and eventually (hopefully) succeed. You can use the experience of working on this problem, and that feeling of success, to remind students that they are capable of solving hard problems when they don't give up.

Students develop resilience when they are given problems that are challenging but not impossible. There is a certain satisfaction in getting to the top of a mountain after a long climb that you do not feel if you take the chair lift. Our classroom culture should be one where it's frowned upon to spoil other students' 'fun' by calling out answers and giving the game away. Students should feel as though they belong to a community of mathematicians who work together in order to solve problems and make sense of the mathematical world around them.

A metacognitive classroom

Perhaps this chapter has given you an appetite for helping your students to be more aware of how metacognitive strategies can help them to solve problems and make connections. So what does a metacognitive classroom look like?

- Students and teachers pose thought-provoking questions.
- The focus is on strategies and methods, explanations and justifications.
- Everyone believes that progress and improvement is possible.
- Everyone values being part of a community of mathematicians.

So, how can we build a classroom culture like this? To influence student behaviour, we have to be explicit about what we value, and praise it when we see it. Why not try setting some lesson objectives that particularly focus on metacognitive skills? Here are some examples:

- We are learning to persevere when we get stuck on a problem.
- In this lesson, we will practise thinking aloud while working on an investigation.
- We are looking at a variety of strategies and learning to determine which is most elegant or efficient.

When you see students who are demonstrating positive metacognitive skills, praise them for it:

- 'Well done, you are looking carefully at what went wrong in order to learn from your mistakes.'
- 'It's great to see you making a plan of what you will do next.'
- 'That's a really good question to ask.'
- 'This group is working really well, they are making sure everyone gets a chance to explain their thoughts.'

Summary

The key points to remember in this chapter are:

- Students are naturally curious. Present them with contexts where they can explore and ask thought-provoking questions.

- Solving problems is a skill that needs to be explicitly taught. Model the behaviours that you wish to foster in your students.

- Give students opportunities to struggle and to succeed, to reflect your belief that every student is capable of making progress.

- Praise students for asking questions, explaining their thinking, justifying their conclusions and reflecting on their own and others' approaches.

Language awareness

9

What is language awareness?

For many students, English is an additional language. It might be their second or perhaps their third language. Depending on the school context, students might be learning all or just some of their subjects through English.

For all students, regardless of whether they are learning through their first language or an additional language, language is a vehicle for learning. It is through language that students access the learning intentions of the lesson and communicate their ideas. It is our responsibility as teachers to ensure that language doesn't present a barrier to learning.

One way to achieve this is to support our colleagues in becoming more language-aware. Language awareness is sensitivity to, and an understanding of, the language demands of our subject and the role these demands play in learning. A language-aware teacher plans strategies and scaffolds the appropriate support to help students overcome these language demands.

Why is it important for teachers of other subjects to be language-aware?

Many teachers are surprised when they receive a piece of written work that suggests a student who has no difficulties in everyday communication has had problems understanding the lesson. Issues arise when teachers assume that students who have attained a high degree of fluency and accuracy in everyday social English therefore have a corresponding level of academic language proficiency. Whether English is a student's first language or an additional language, students need time and the appropriate support to become proficient in academic language. This is the language that they are mostly exposed to in school and will be required to reproduce themselves. It will also scaffold their ability to access higher order thinking skills and improve levels of attainment.

What are the challenges of language awareness?

Many teachers of non-language subjects worry that there is no time to factor language support into their lessons, or that language is something they know little about. Some teachers may think that language support is not their role. However, we need to work with these teachers to create inclusive classrooms where all students can access the curriculum and where barriers to learning are reduced as much as possible. An increased awareness of the language needs of students aims to reduce any obstacles that learning through an additional language might present.

This doesn't mean that all teachers need to know the names of grammatical structures or need to be able to use the appropriate linguistic labels. What it does mean is that we all need to understand the challenges our students face, including their language level, and plan some strategies to help them overcome these challenges. These strategies do not need to take a lot of additional time and should eventually become integral to our process of planning, teaching and reflecting on our practice. We may need to support other teachers so that they are clear about the vocabulary and language that is specific to their subject, and how to teach, reinforce and develop it.

Introduction

We think, we listen, we talk, we read and we often take this for granted. In this chapter, we are going to unpick how we communicate with our students, and how they communicate with us and with each other. How language is used in our classrooms has a massive impact on what our students learn and how they learn it.

To help us become aware of how language is being used in our classrooms, we are going to focus on four key considerations:

- Who is doing the talking:
  -whole-class interaction
  -group work
  -teacher-student dialogue?
- Why are they talking?
- What are they talking about?
- How are they talking?

For each of these, we will look at how we can support students who may have difficulties with language that get in the way of their mathematical success.

Who is doing the talking?

David Rooke, when he was the Chair of the Association of Teachers of Mathematics (ATM), said that for him, the one word that can sum up real teaching is listening, to what students say to the teacher, to what they say to each other and to the silences.

Yet, in many classrooms, teachers can be observed doing a great deal of talking and not enough listening! Let's look at the balance of communication in whole-class interaction, group work and teacher-student dialogue.

Whole-class interaction

This can sometimes play out as a game of 'ping pong', where the teacher speaks, a student responds, the teacher speaks, another student responds, and so on. Often this results in a swift exchange between the teacher and the more confident students. If your classroom becomes a game of 'ping pong', consider switching to 'volleyball', where the teacher speaks, a student responds, another student responds, another student responds, the teacher speaks, and back it goes to the students. An advantage of being part of a 'volleyball' team, as opposed to playing 'ping pong', is the expectation that everyone will contribute and participate in the game.

Teacher Tip

Some teachers choose to have a 'no-hands-up' policy, which ensures that a wider range of students are involved in answering questions. To ensure that the selection process is both fair and random, some teachers write the names of their students on lolly sticks, to then pick out of a jar. This means that students who have misconceptions and are perhaps uncertain will contribute more often to the conversation. This has two distinct advantages. It will give the teacher a much clearer picture of students' understanding, and ensure that difficulties are addressed.

In 'ping pong' students often look to the teacher to judge the merits of what has been said and this leads to a classroom culture in which students become very dependent on teachers' judgements. In 'volleyball', teachers can relinquish that responsibility, allowing students to assess and respond to the contributions that are made. This is an important aspect of students belonging to a mathematical community that supports and relies on each other. What is more, students get used to listening to their peers as well as the teacher and in a classroom with bilingual students, a student can switch languages to clarify something quickly with their peers so that mathematical discussion is not hampered by a language barrier.

Group work

Students working collaboratively in pairs or small groups allows for multiple conversations to take place at the same time. Here again, ensuring that everybody's voice is heard is of crucial importance.

Teacher Tip

A common strategy used by teachers is 'Think/Pair/Share' where a question is asked, everybody is given some thinking time before being asked to talk to their partners, and finally they are invited to share their thoughts with the rest of the class. The enforced thinking time makes it more likely that everyone will have something to contribute to the discussion. The paired work allows students to rehearse and refine their emergent thinking in a safe environment. If the teacher moves around the classroom at this stage to listen to conversations, it will reveal to them what the students are thinking. This will enable the teacher to make an informed decision when selecting who should report back in the 'Share' stage. The teacher can then ensure that a range of different perspectives are aired for consideration. This strategy offers new opportunities for students' development each and every time it is used in the classroom. Eventually your aim should be for all students to be confident in their ability to communicate their ideas to the whole class.

Teacher Tip

John Mason has suggested a mathematical version of 'Think/Pair/Share' in which the challenge is to:

'Convince yourself'

'Convince a friend'

'Convince an enemy'.

See Chapter 6 **Active learning** for an in-depth discussion of using Mason's mathematical powers in the classroom.

Teacher-student dialogue

In a busy classroom, teachers can only spend a limited amount of time talking to individual students, so careful consideration needs to be given to these interactions so that they can be as purposeful and productive as possible.

Students can become rather dependent on their teachers. They often use one-to-one interactions to confirm that what they're doing is right, to simplify the problem, or to get the teacher to do some of the thinking for them.

Teacher Tip

To escape this unhelpful behaviour, some teachers choose to 'question answers' rather than 'answer questions'. As the students become accustomed to this way of working, they become more independent, and resourceful in turning to their peers as a first port of call.

Why are they talking?

'Language plays an essential part in the formulation and expression of mathematical ideas' – The Cockcroft report (para. 306).

We have already written about the importance of helping students to organise and refine their ideas. Now we will move on to explore why we ask students to talk in their Mathematics lessons.

In Mathematics, we try to move from the particular to the general, and encourage students to:

- explore
- notice
- describe
- conjecture
- generalise
- justify
- prove.

None of which can be done without language!

The language associated with each of these activities is different and so it is important that students are exposed to the full range.

For example, you could say 'Choose several sets of five consecutive numbers and add them together.' and the students might say:

'I got 40, 25 and 100 ...' (*describing*)

'I think that five consecutive numbers always add up to multiples of 5 ...' (*noticing/conjecturing*)

'$a + (a + 1) + (a + 2) + (a +3) + (a +4) = 5a + 10 = 5(a +2)$'

so five consecutive numbers do add up to a multiple of 5.' (*justifying/proving*)

Alternatively, you could say 'Can you write a unit fraction as the difference of two unit fractions?' and the students might say:

'Yes, $\dfrac{1}{6} = \dfrac{1}{2} - \dfrac{1}{3}$,'

'Yes, $\dfrac{1}{20} = \dfrac{1}{4} - \dfrac{1}{5}$,'

'Yes, $\dfrac{1}{30} = \dfrac{1}{5} - \dfrac{1}{6} \ldots$' (*describing*)

'I think that any unit fraction in which the denominator is the product of two consecutive numbers can be written as the difference of two unit fractions ...' (*conjecturing*)

$$
\begin{aligned}
\text{'}1/n(n + 1) &= \frac{1}{n} - \frac{1}{(n + 1)} \\
&= \frac{(n + 1)}{n(n + 1)} - \frac{n}{n(n + 1)} \\
&= \frac{(n + 1 - n)}{n(n + 1)} \\
&= \frac{1}{n(n + 1)}
\end{aligned}
$$

so all unit fractions in which the denominator is the product of two consecutive numbers can be written as the difference of two unit fractions.' (*justifying/proving*)

You need to ensure that the language you use in the classroom reflects the richness of the mathematical activity that you'd like your students to engage with.

You need your students to be able to describe, explain, conjecture and prove, and in order to do so they need to be exposed to the vocabulary that will prepare them for these different 'mathematical registers'.

Teacher Tip

Model the sort of language that mathematicians use at each stage of the process of generalising. When sharing conjectures, draw attention to students who express their ideas in a particularly mathematical way, or using correct mathematical vocabulary. The following sentence starters might be helpful as prompt cards or a poster:

I think this because…

If this is true, then…

I know that the next one is… because…

When I tried… I noticed that…

The pattern looks like…

What are they talking about?

Dialogue in the classroom sometimes involves vocabulary that is specifically mathematical (e.g. hypotenuse, vector, trigonometry and parallel) and sometimes involves vocabulary that has an additional mathematical meaning to its everyday use (e.g. face, mean, takeaway, volume, power and difference).

Teacher tip

As teachers, we need to remember that some of the specifically mathematical vocabulary may be unfamiliar to many students, and that we may be misunderstood when we use words that have more than one meaning. It can be helpful for students to create their own mathematical glossary/dictionary while they are working or at the end of each lesson. Allocating time to review new vocabulary and make sense of it in their own words will help to support their understanding and embed subject specific language into their thinking for future use.

It is important to share pertinent mathematical vocabulary sensitively and at appropriate times with students. Allowing them to express their thoughts in their own words is crucial when encouraging students to share their ideas, but at some point more rigorous language will be required.

We also need to ensure that students are familiar with standard mathematical conventions. Confusion can arise when:

- Similar combinations of elements do not always imply identical operations – for example, 45 is forty plus five, whereas 4a is four multiplied by a.
- The spatial arrangement of numbers and symbols carries different meanings – for example, 3^5 is not the same as 35.
- Symbols have different uses – for example, $48°$ (the angle) means something different from $18°C$ (the temperature).

(Access and Engagement in Mathematics, 2002)

Teacher Tip

Having displays that include the relevant vocabulary and conventions for current topics is a helpful way of supporting and developing students' growing mathematical lexicon. For example, a poster for each year group, showing key words that will be used in that year, allows students at the end of the lesson to look at the poster and pick out the words they learned that day. They can also look ahead to see some of the words they will be learning in the future, and perhaps spot some that they already know!

Dialogue in the classroom sometimes involves justifications and proof, which in Mathematics has to be logically set out so that there is no room for dispute. We need to train our students so that they can present rigorous arguments in a way that is acceptable to the mathematical community.

At an early stage, we can encourage students to develop their mathematical reasoning by carrying out activities like the 'Always, Sometimes, Never' task that we described in the Chapter 7 **Assessment for Learning**.

▣ LESSON IDEA ONLINE 9.1: KITE IN A SQUARE

To introduce students to rigorous proof, we can offer them scrambled up statements, which they need to order into a mathematically logical chain.

The NRICH problem 'Kite in a Square' (www.nrich.maths.org/kiteinasquare) offers such an opportunity. Students are given the square shown in Figure 9.1, told that M is

➔

the midpoint of AB and asked to work out what fraction of the total area is shaded.

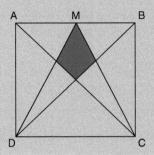

Figure 9.1

The statements that follow relate to the annotated diagram shown in Figure 9.2. They have been muddled up and students are asked to put them in the correct order.

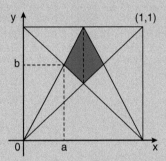

Figure 9.2

The shaded area is made up of two congruent triangles, one of which has vertices $\left(\frac{1}{3},\frac{2}{3}\right)$, $\left(\frac{1}{2},\frac{1}{2}\right)$, $\left(\frac{1}{2},1\right)$.	A
The line joining $(0,0)$ to $\left(\frac{1}{2},1\right)$ has equation $y = 2x$.	B
Area of the triangle $= \frac{1}{2}\left(\frac{1}{2}\times\frac{1}{6}\right) = \frac{1}{24}$	C
The line joining $(0,1)$ to $(1,0)$ has equation $y = 1 - x$.	D

→

Therefore the shaded area is $2 \times \frac{1}{24} = \frac{1}{12}$.	E
The point (a, b) is at the intersection of the lines $y = 2x$ and $y = 1 - x$.	F
Consider a unit square drawn on a coordinate grid.	G
The perpendicular height of the triangle is $\frac{1}{2} - \frac{1}{3} = \frac{1}{6}$.	H
So $a = \frac{1}{3}, b = \frac{2}{3}$.	I
The line joining $(0,0)$ to $(1,1)$ has equation $y = x$.	J

This task also contains two other sets of muddled up statements that tackle the same problem using different approaches (one uses Pythagoras and one uses similar figures).

By presenting students with a complete proof, albeit one that has been muddled up, you are modelling the language and symbolic notation that they will be expected to produce when writing their own proofs. You could use a proof sorter activity with a class and then later ask them to recreate the proof for themselves without looking, assessing them on the accuracy with which they use mathematical language and symbols.

How are they talking?

We know that language is essential for students developing their mathematical understanding, so we need to ensure that the quality of the talking and listening that goes on in the classroom is productive and purposeful. This doesn't necessarily happen naturally, so some teachers find it useful to have some rules that govern how students communicate with each other. Neil Mercer suggests the following:

- All students must contribute: no one member says too much or too little.
- Every contribution treated with respect: listen thoughtfully.
- Group must achieve consensus: work at resolving differences.
- Every suggestion/assertion has to be justified: arguments must include reasons.

These ground rules need to be considered alongside an awareness that the amount of time we give students to think about questions has a significant positive impact. 'Waiting time' can take place after the teacher asks a question, at a pause during a student's response, after a student responds or after a significant statement from the teacher. Research shows the following effects when these 'waiting times' are increased from 0.9 to more than 3 seconds:

- The length of student response increased.
- More responses were supported by logical argument.
- There were an increased number of speculative responses.
- The number of questions asked by students increased.
- Student–to–student exchanges increased.
- Failures to respond decreased.
- 'Disciplinary moves' decreased (that is, a student being moved to a different seat in the class as a means of managing their behaviour).
- The variety of students participating increased.
- The number of unsolicited and appropriate contributions increased.
- Student confidence increased.

Clearly if the questions teachers ask are meaningful and require considered responses, then time in which to think will be required. By increasing 'waiting time', teachers can implicitly give the message that speed is not required to develop as a good mathematician.

The opportunities so far listed in this chapter apply to all students, but, in addition to these, EAL students find it beneficial to be encouraged to rehearse thoughts in their first language initially. For such students, having access to a mathematical dictionary or vocabulary list of key words for a particular topic can support the communication of emergent ideas, understanding of concepts and formulation of questions needed for clarification. Visual representations including diagrams, models and manipulatives can be very helpful in exposing or illustrating mathematical structures to students whose fluency with English might otherwise be a barrier to a verbal or written explanation.

That Mathematics is a truly universal language can be seen most clearly when teachers and students of different nationalities and tongues come together. If a common number system is shared, such as Hindu-Arabic numerals, much exploration, exposition and resultant excitement can be shared through the conventions of mathematical notation and the meaning it conveys that transcends mere 'language' as we might ordinarily think of it.

For example, in the task 'Sandwiches' (www.nrich.maths.org/sandwiches), students are invited to arrange pairs of digit cards so that between the two 1s there is exactly one other digit, between the two 2s there are exactly two other digits and so on. Teachers and students who share no common language have successfully worked on this task together using pointing, counting and excited nods!

We know that many children are anxious about their potential to learn Mathematics and many adults report having had very bad experiences of learning Mathematics themselves, so we need to ensure that our students feel safe and secure when they come into our lessons if they are to function productively. Carol Dweck's research, which was mentioned in Chapter 8 **Metacognition**, suggests that not only is it important for students to have a growth mindset, but for their teachers to have a flexible idea of their students' capabilities.

Teacher Tip

A Mathematics teacher was concerned that many of his students said 'I can't do this', so he created a poster with just one word on it. The word was 'YET' and every time a student said 'I can't do this', he pointed at the poster and invited them to say instead 'I can't do this yet'. Language and its power to influence how we feel was being taken very seriously in this classroom.

Another Mathematics teacher has a different poster in her classroom: 'Whether you think you can, or whether you think you can't, you're probably right.' She also points at the poster whenever students exhibit a fixed mindset.

To develop a non-threatening environment for students, where they feel safe in contributing to discussion, try using the phrase 'I am interested in knowing anything you know.'

We need to think carefully about how we communicate with our students. The language that we use, the tone we adopt, and how we communicate our expectations, all have a significant impact on our students' attitudes and performance.

Summary

Language is essential for giving students opportunities to talk themselves into understanding. Give careful consideration to the following:

- Who is doing the talking?

- Why are they talking?

- What are they talking about?

- How are they talking?

You can influence all of these aspects of classroom communication, which can have a significant impact on students' learning.

10 | Inclusive education

What is inclusive education?

Individual differences among students will always exist; our challenge as teachers is to see these not as problems to be fixed but as opportunities to enrich and make learning accessible for all. Inclusion is an effort to make sure all students receive whatever specially designed instruction and support they need to succeed as learners.

An inclusive teacher welcomes all students and finds ways to accept and accommodate each individual student. An inclusive teacher identifies existing barriers that limit access to learning, then finds solutions and strategies to remove or reduce those barriers. Some barriers to inclusion are visible; others are hidden or difficult to recognise.

Barriers to inclusion might be the lack of educational resources available for teachers or an inflexible curriculum that does not take into account the learning differences that exist among all learners, across all ages. We also need to encourage students to understand each others' barriers, or this itself may become a barrier to learning.

Students may experience challenges because of any one or a combination of the following:

- behavioural and social skill difficulties
- communication or language disabilities
- concentration difficulties
- conflict in the home or that caused by political situations or national emergency
- executive functions, such as difficulties in understanding, planning and organising
- hearing impairments, acquired congenitally or through illness or injury
- literacy and language difficulties
- numeracy difficulties
- physical or neurological impairments, which may or may not be visible
- visual impairments, ranging from mild to severe.

We should be careful, however, not to label a student and create further barriers in so doing, particularly if we ourselves are not qualified to make a diagnosis. Each child is unique but it is our management of their learning environment that will decide the extent of the barrier and the need for it to be a factor. We need to be aware of a child's readiness to learn and their readiness for school.

Why is inclusive education important?

Teachers need to find ways to welcome all students and organise their teaching so that each student gets a learning experience that makes engagement and success possible. We should create a good match between what we teach and how we teach it, and what the student needs and is capable of. We need not only to ensure access but also make sure each student receives the support and individual attention that result in meaningful learning.

What are the challenges of an inclusive classroom?

Some students may have unexpected barriers. Those who consistently do well in class may not perform in exams, or those who are strong at writing may be weaker when speaking. Those who are considered to be the brightest students may also have barriers to learning. Some students may be working extra hard to compensate for barriers they prefer to keep hidden; some students may suddenly reveal limitations in their ability to learn, using the techniques they have been taught. We need to be aware of all corners of our classroom, be open and put ourselves in our students' shoes.

We can all learn Mathematics

Mathematics is a subject with the potential to inspire all learners.
It touches all of our lives, both inside and outside of the classroom.
Mathematics offers a language for understanding the world around us,
from the spiral patterns we observe on pine cones to the wonderful
curving roof design of the Olympic swimming pool for the London
2012 Olympics. Mathematical models enable meteorologists to predict
the weather days or even weeks in advance, they allow scientists to
explore the prevention of the spread of infectious diseases and they
unleash the creative potential of architects and engineers as they design
our 21st-century world. Every student should experience moments of
awe and wonder during their mathematical journey. The challenge is for
us to adapt our lesson plans, teaching approaches and classroom ethos
to ensure that every student has access to this essential subject, and can
participate at the right level.

A growth mindset

Carol Dweck (2008) found that students make more progress when they
are taught by teachers with a growth mindset than when they are taught
by teachers with a fixed mindset (see Chapter 8 **Metacognition**). We
need to establish clear conditions for our students to make progress in our
Mathematics classrooms, and a growth mindset is an essential component:
teachers and students must believe that progress is possible. 'I can't do
this' must become 'I can't do this yet'. We need to focus on, and help
our students develop, the mathematical skills and habits that will nurture
young mathematicians. Our planning and feedback needs to ensure that
students work in an environment where everyone believes that success is
possible if students work hard and collaborate with each other. Students
need to experience activities that demand resilience, perseverance and
resourcefulness so they can experience the wonderfully uplifting feeling
we get when we solve a challenging problem. In our inclusive classrooms,
it is crucial that we look for potential in our students and build on their
current skills and capabilities, rather than just focus on what they cannot

do. All students can experience success, often at different levels, so it is important to plan for these successes. Fostering a 'can do' atmosphere can become infectious, students becoming more willing to try and try again. Modelling and valuing such an approach is very important. Carefully chosen activities can help foster a growth mindset, so our chosen problems must start by being accessible and engaging and, as they become more challenging, encourage students to persevere and collaborate so that they can make progress and experience success.

Low-threshold, high-ceiling tasks

It can be tempting to plan different activities for different groups of students in our classes according to our perceptions of their needs and capabilities, but that may not always be the best approach. Differentiating in this way can be a planning nightmare and it can make it difficult to monitor progress and offer support to students during lessons. Instead, it can be more effective to identify a single starting activity that can be adapted during the lesson using our professional judgement. Such activities are often referred to as low-threshold, high-ceiling (LTHC) tasks. The low-threshold means that most students should find the task initially accessible, and the high-ceiling means that the level of challenge can be extended for students as required. LTHC activities offer an alternative way of structuring our lessons that does not set limits on what our students might achieve in those lessons.

The best LTHC activities are rich activities; mathematical tasks that are thought provoking and engaging for students, and offer choice and opportunities to progress in a variety of ways.

▣ LESSON IDEA ONLINE 10.1: ODDS AND EVENS

'Odds and Evens' (www.nrich.maths.org/oddsandevens) is an excellent activity that illustrates the key features of LTHC tasks (see Figure 10.1).

→

Here is a set A of numbered balls used for a game:

To play the game, the balls are mixed up and two balls are randomly picked out together. For example:

The numbers on the balls are added together: 4 + 5 = 9.

If the total is even, you win. If the total is odd, you lose.

How can you decide whether the game is fair?

Figure 10.1

Start by showing students how the game is played using counters in a bag numbered 2, 3, 4, 5 and 6, or using the online activity. Play the game a few times so that students have a feel for the game but don't have sufficient results to draw firm conclusions about the probabilities. Then ask them to decide whether they think the game is fair, and ask them to come up with convincing arguments to justify their conclusions.

Students will be required to work systematically to derive all possible results, and to record their work in a useful way (see Figure 10.2). Students can then move to comparing the fairness of different versions of the game.

2,3

2,4 ✓

2,5

2,6 ✓

3,4

3,5 ✓

3,6

4,5

4,6 ✓

5,6

	2	3	4	5	6
2	X	5	6	7	8
3	5	X	7	8	9
4	6	7	X	9	10
5	7	8	9	X	11
6	8	9	10	11	X

	2	3	4	5	6
2	X	O	E	O	E
3	O	X	O	E	O
4	E	O	X	O	E
5	O	E	O	X	O
6	E	O	E	O	X

Figure 10.2

→

Some students may move on to working together to develop a conjecture about the number of odd and even balls needed for a fair game. This may require them to generate lots of data, which they can sort and analyse and use to justify their conclusions. The activity moves from experimental probability (low-threshold) to theoretical probability (high-ceiling), encouraging collaborative work and requiring students to predict, analyse and justify.

Teacher Tip

To make the most of 'Odds and Evens', you can ask:

- How can we decide whether a game is fair?
- What are the most efficient methods for recording possible combinations?
- How can we make this difficult task (of finding a fair game) more manageable?

Fostering a community of mathematicians

How often do we give our students opportunities to work collaboratively? Many rich mathematical tasks have been designed with group work in mind, and they offer excellent opportunities for mixed-ability teaching. Jo Boaler has written about the teachers at a school whose students made significant progress and reported very positive attitudes towards Mathematics, after being introduced to a group work approach known as 'Complex Instruction' (Boaler, 2009). The teachers stressed to their students that they all 'had strengths in different areas and that everyone had something important to offer when working on Maths'. The teachers ensured that students collaborated by giving them non-routine problems that they could not solve by simply reproducing using earlier methods. 'Complex Instruction' offers students an insight into how mathematicians often work.

Encouraging varied approaches

How can we increase the number of successful students in our classes? When Boaler (2009) compared teaching approaches and attainment levels in two different schools, she reported that in the 'Complex Instruction' school 'many more students were successful, because there were many more ways to be successful'. In our inclusive classrooms we will want to encourage a variety of approaches, so we must select activities that can be tackled in a variety of ways.

☑ **LESSON IDEA ONLINE 10.2: TEMPERATURE**
nrich.maths.org/temperature

Temperature

Temperature is often measured in Celsius (°C) or Fahrenheit (°F).

The freezing point of water is 0°C or 32°F.

The boiling point of water is 100°C or 212°F.

Is there a temperature at which the Celsius and Fahrenheit readings are the same?

nrich.maths.org

Figure 10.3

This task brings together Science and Mathematics, making it an engaging activity for those students who are drawn more towards the sciences than to Mathematics (see Figure 10.3).

Allowing some discussion time at the start, and drawing on students' prior knowledge about the boiling and freezing points of water in both Celsius and Fahrenheit, may be a good way to start. Asking 'What other information can you deduce from these temperature facts?' and offering the class some time to discuss their ideas in pairs, may be a good way to ease students into the problem. Possible responses might include:

'50°C = 122°F because it's halfway between.'

'200°C = 392°F because it's another 180°F.'

'A temperature increase of 100°C is the same as a temperature increase of 180°F.'

An important element of developing an inclusive approach is valuing everyone's contributions. You can encourage this by asking 'Can you use each other's ideas to deduce any more information about the temperature scales?'.

Figure 10.4 shows the initial thoughts from one group of students:

Every time you go down 5 degrees in the Celsius scale, you go down 9 degrees in the Fahrenheit scale.

```
  0°C = 32°F
 −5°C = 32°F −9 = 23°F
−10°C = 23°F −9 = 14°F
−15°C = 14°F −9 = 5°F
−20°C = 5°F −9 = −4°F
−25°C = −4°F −9 = −13°F
−30°C = −13°F −9 = −22°F
−40°C = −31°F −9 = −40°F
−40°C = −40°F
```

Figure 10.4

Once students have had a chance to deduce some more information, they may be ready for the main question: 'Is there a temperature where the reading in Celsius is the same as the reading in Fahrenheit?'

How might our students present their solutions? Some students might choose to adopt an algebraic approach to a solution using the conversion formula for Celsius and Fahrenheit (see Figure 10.5).

Let x be the temperature where Fahranheit and Celsius are equal.

$$x = \frac{9}{5}x + 32$$

$$5x = 9x + 160$$

$$-4x = 160a$$

$$x = -40a$$

Therefore –40 Celsius = –40 Farenheit

Figure 10.5

Other students might prefer to present their solutions using a more visual approach using graphs (see Figure 10.6).

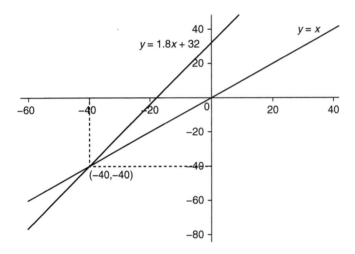

Figure 10.6

In each case, what really mattered was the thinking behind each approach. The different solutions offer an opportunity to discuss the effectiveness of the different strategies and the reasoning behind them. This way, everyone's contribution can be valued and classrooms can become much more flexible working and learning environments.

Teacher Tip

Prepare a resource bank of different solutions to problems, for use as prompts with other classes. Students can choose which solutions they prefer and why, and perhaps experiment with trying out different approaches to their favoured ones.

When students get stuck on problems, it is important that they can support each other to overcome obstacles. Many students are happy sharing their ideas and approaches, but less confident students may be a little reticent. It is important that we allow students to share their thoughts and ideas in a variety of ways that do not put the less confident speakers under undue stress.

A very popular way to encourage the sharing of ideas is through 'posters':

☑ **LESSON IDEA ONLINE 10.3: M, M AND M**
(www.nrich.maths.org/mmandm)

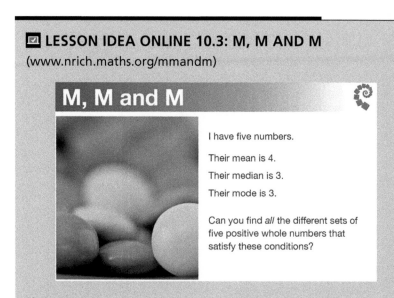

M, M and M

I have five numbers.

Their mean is 4.

Their median is 3.

Their mode is 3.

Can you find *all* the different sets of five positive whole numbers that satisfy these conditions?

Figure 10.7

Hand out a large sheet of paper to each group of students so that they can annotate it as they work on their problem together. At some point during the lesson, ask the students to visit the other tables and study their posters. It is fascinating to see the immediate impact of such an approach, some students look for confirmation that their approach is the 'right one', others check that they have followed a similar approach, or scan for help with a particular problem they are struggling with. Once the students have had sufficient time to visit each group, encourage them to return to their own tables and reflect on what they have seen, and consider editing/improving/altering their own work in the light of it.

This inclusive approach illustrates what it is really like to work as a mathematician: sharing ideas, collaborating, explaining and justifying, involving students who offer different approaches. It allows students to change their approach if necessary and to see errors and mistakes as an important part of the learning process.

Celebrating skills beyond Mathematics

One highly effective way of engaging students in Mathematics is by drawing upon their skills and interests in other subjects. When we considered the 'Temperature' activity, we mentioned that students who were interested in Science might find the question interesting. Sport is also important to many students, and it can offer rich resources for teaching a variety of mathematical topics. By selecting contexts or topics that the students enjoy and are good at, many students will have opportunities to succeed and offer support and guidance to other students.

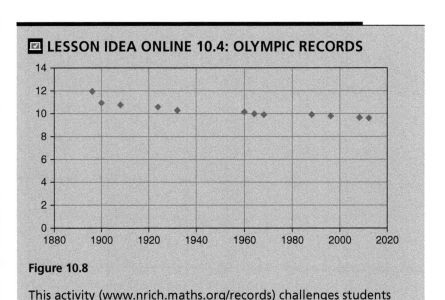

▣ LESSON IDEA ONLINE 10.4: OLYMPIC RECORDS

Figure 10.8

This activity (www.nrich.maths.org/records) challenges students to match ten athletics events to ten graphs showing how their Olympic records have changed over time. Show your students →

the graph in Figure 10.8, and ask them what they think it might represent. Most students will quickly infer that the *x*-axis displays Olympic years and the *y*-axis is time in seconds. However, can they deduce what is actually being measured? At this point the knowledge of the more sporting members of your class will be appreciated. Although many students will insist that the graph shows the 100 m records over time, how confident are they that it represents the men's record rather than the women's record? Or does it represent the 110 m hurdles rather than the 100 m sprint? Giving students an opportunity to share their experiences and knowledge celebrates their skills, promotes inclusivity and makes strong links between Mathematics and the world of sport, into which many students are immersed.

This type of activity allows students to develop arguments and counter-arguments. How do they know whether a graph represents a track event or a field event? Can they explain why some graphs have no data from the early 20th century? Why are there gaps in the graphs in the middle of the 20th century? Challenge students to explain why there was a significant improvement in the men's long jump record in 1968, and a dip in the javelin record in 1986.

Maximising use of digital technologies

Some of your students will have particular needs, which you can address through the careful application of digital technologies. Graphic software, digital recorders, digital cameras and visualisers are all useful equipment for classrooms that aim to be inclusive.

The use of graphic software is a bonus for students with motor control issues, because they can quickly sketch and review graphs to a high standard. Their focus can remain on the Mathematics being taught rather than on issues associated with manipulating their pencil, paper and ruler. Software packages such as GeoGebra and Desmos can facilitate an inclusive approach. See Chapter 11 **Teaching with digital technologies** for an in-depth discussion of the use of digital technology in the classroom.

Likewise, students who experience difficulties with writing or oral presentations may prefer to use digital technologies to record their ideas. Many smartphones now incorporate high-quality voice recorders, but take care to conform to school policies regarding the acceptable use of mobile phones on school grounds.

Focus on what students *can* do

There are two more effective ways in which to support students so that they can participate fully in classroom activities. One involves working with their families, the other requires a slightly different approach to lesson planning. Let's consider working with families first. If a student has specific needs in a Mathematics classroom, it can be time-consuming to arrange their additional support. However, their families may have much more experience in meeting their needs, you may find it very useful to arrange a meeting with them to discuss suitable support.

A second approach involves working with other adults in your school. Too often we tend to 'reinvent the wheel', devising approaches that other colleagues have realised would be useful in their own lessons, and already adopted. Quite often, students with specific needs have a named adult, or paperwork, outlining recommended support. By working closely with that adult, and reviewing the relevant paperwork, we can draw on a much wider repertoire of effective strategies than we might have initially considered for our student. This works really well when we want to make connections to the student's interests outside the classroom; their adult helper may already know activities that interest the student that you could include in your lessons. By sharing planning in advance of their lessons, an adult helper may have time to consider ways in which to adapt them so that they meet the needs of the student.

Summary

At some point in their school career, almost every student will require additional support. Some students will require it for longer, a few will require it in every lesson throughout their school life. We can promote inclusive classrooms, in which all our students can participate, when we:

- foster a growth mindset

- choose low-threshold, high-ceiling activities

- encourage different approaches to solutions

- explain that it is all right to get stuck

- celebrate skills beyond Mathematics

- focus on what our students can do

- work with other adults.

These strategies help us cater for the differing needs of our students, offering every one of them the opportunity to participate and succeed in our Mathematics lessons.

Teaching with digital technologies

11

11

What are digital technologies?

Digital technologies enable our students to access a wealth of up-to-date digital resources, collaborate locally and globally, curate existing material and create new material. They include electronic devices and tools that manage and manipulate information and data.

Why use digital technologies in the classroom?

When used successfully, digital technologies have the potential to transform teaching and learning. The effective use of technology in the classroom encourages active learning, knowledge construction, inquiry and exploration among students. It should enhance an existing task or provide opportunities to do things that could not be done without it. It can also enhance the role of assessment, providing new ways for students to demonstrate evidence of learning.

New technologies are redefining relationships and enabling new opportunities. But there are also risks, so we should encourage our students to be knowledgeable about and responsible in their use of technology. Integrating technology into our teaching helps prepare students for a future rooted in an increasingly digitised world.

What are the challenges of using digital technologies?

The key to ensuring that technology is used effectively is to remember that it is simply a resource, and not an end in itself. As with the use of all resources, the key is not to start with the resource itself, but to start with what you want the student to learn. We need to think carefully about why and how to use technologies as well as evaluating their efficiency and effectiveness.

If students are asked to use digital technologies as part of their homework, it is important that all students are able to access the relevant technology outside school. A school needs to think about a response to any 'digital divide', because if technology is 'adding value', then all students need to be able to benefit. Some schools choose to make resources available to borrow or use in school, or even loan devices to students.

Safety for students and teachers is a key challenge for schools and it is important to consider issues such as the prevention of cyber-bullying, the hacking of personal information, access to illegal or banned materials and distractions from learning. As technology changes, schools and teachers need to adapt and implement policies and rules.

One of the greatest pitfalls is for a teacher to feel that they are not skilled technologists, and therefore not to try. Creative things can be done with simple technology, and a highly effective teacher who knows very little about technology can often achieve much more than a less effective teacher who is a technology expert. Knowing how to use technology is not the same as knowing how to teach with it.

Introduction

'Technology is an essential tool for learning Mathematics in the 21st century, and all schools must ensure that all their students have access to technology' (National Council of Teachers of Mathematics [NCTM], 2008).

The availability of digital technology means that students today can learn Mathematics in a very different way from how they might have learned it 30 or 40 years ago. In the past, there was an emphasis on accurately performing standard calculations that can now be done easily by computers. In fact, virtually everybody carries a calculator around with them these days in the form of a mobile phone. This is not to say that children don't need to be able to add up any more, but our teaching of Mathematics needs to use the tools that are now available – we need to teach our students how and when to use technology so that they use it appropriately.

The way that Mathematics is done in society has also changed. Professional mathematicians have always used the cutting edge technology of their time to support their work, and if we want our classrooms to reflect real Mathematics, we need to give our students opportunities to integrate technology into what they do. This doesn't mean that you have to plan lots of extra lessons in an already stretched curriculum – using digital tools can save time and be a huge asset in supporting students' learning.

There are many ways to incorporate digital technologies into our Mathematics teaching. This chapter explores briefly some ways in which teachers can demonstrate the use of technology, and then focuses in much more detail on how students can get to grips with using technology for themselves.

Teacher demonstration

Many classrooms now have interactive whiteboards and projectors, and these can prove to be of real benefit to students' understanding. At the beginning of a lesson, we can project an image, video or interactive environment on to the board to set the context for the lesson.

For example, the image shows an environment for exploring Mathematics on dotty grids (see Figure 11.1), where we might ask:

- Can you draw squares using each of these lines as a side?
- Can you draw squares using each of these lines as a diagonal?

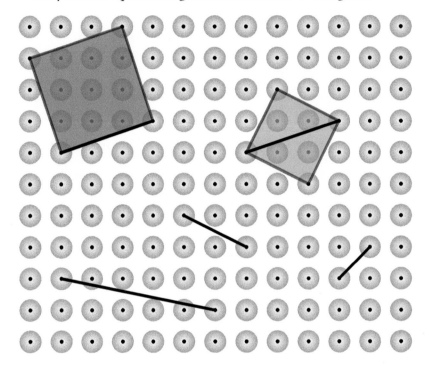

Figure 11.1

The interactive environment provides a shared focal point to set the scene of the problem, and then later a space where students can come out to the front of the class and share their ideas.

Teacher Tip

A well-crafted set of slides can add value to a lesson, but be careful of over-preparing. Slides can be used effectively to present a problem or highlight an idea or concept. The danger comes when the slides dictate what goes on in the lesson and prevent you from being responsive to your students.

We will explore later on how students can use dynamic geometry, spreadsheets and graphing software to explore problems, but sometimes you may wish to use these tools to demonstrate an idea. The free program Desmos (www.desmos.com/calculator) offers a quick and easy way to plot graphs of several functions on the same axes, with sliders so you can vary coefficients. At the start of a topic about gradient of straight lines, you could plot $y = ax + b$ and invite students to make predictions about what will happen as you vary a and b. They then move the sliders to see whether their predictions are right.

Teacher Tip

The GeoGebra website has a huge wealth of free interactive demonstrations on a variety of topics that you can download and show to your students. For example, if you search for 'Pythagoras Proof' you can find many different interactive proofs of Pythagoras's Theorem that use slides and animations to demonstrate the theorem without lots of algebra. (www.geogebra.org/materials).

As well as general mathematical software such as GeoGebra and Desmos, there are many interactive apps available online for introducing topics or offering consolidation practice. You can use these as a whole-class teaching tool as well as for students to work on individually.

☑ LESSON IDEA ONLINE 11.1: SHIFTING TIMES TABLES

The NRICH problem 'Shifting Times Tables' (www.nrich.maths.org/shifting) offers an interactive way of introducing linear sequences and *n*th term rules. The app generates terms from a random sequence and invites students to work out the times table and the amount by which it has been shifted. There are four levels of difficulty. The following are examples of Level 2 and 3 questions:

- Level 2 example: 14, 26, 38, 50, 62 – answer : 12 times table shifted up by 2
- Level 3 example: 171, 154, 239, 205, 86 – answer: 17 times table shifted up by 1

→

You could start the lesson by working on a couple of examples as a class, and then once students get the idea they could work in pairs until they have a strategy and can work out the times table and shift every time. Then bring the class together and generate some more examples so students can demonstrate their strategies. The benefit of using interactive apps like this is that students get instant feedback about whether they are right or wrong and can try as many examples as they need in order to figure out a strategy. You might suggest that once they get five questions right in a row, they are ready to move up to the next level.

Here are some other NRICH tasks that can be used in a similar way:

- 'Dozens' (www.nrich.maths.org/dozens)
- 'Factors and Multiples' game (www.nrich.maths.org/factorsandmultiples)
- 'Charlie's Delightful Machine' (www.nrich.maths.org/delightful)
- 'Square It' (www.nrich.maths.org/squareit)

Students at the controls

By far the most powerful way that digital technology can have an impact on our students is by letting them use it themselves! If we see our Mathematics classrooms as places where young people can learn to think and work like mathematicians, then we need to give them opportunities to use digital tools alongside pen and paper. Ken Ruthven proposed a model of student learning in Mathematics that consists of three stages: exploration, codification and consolidation. Rather than beginning a new topic with an explanation by the teacher, students are first given time to be playful and to explore a new context for themselves. The teacher's role is to then pull ideas together, using students' insights and findings, and introduce them to the appropriate vocabulary and notation. Using digital tools can widen the scope of student exploration by letting them look at many more examples than would be possible with pencil and paper alone. Digital technology frees students from time-consuming calculations and drawings so that they can use their energy to engage with more mathematically interesting ideas.

Approaches to learning and teaching Mathematics

The current generation of schoolchildren are often described as digital natives, as they have grown up surrounded by technology. This provides us with both an opportunity and a challenge. If we can tap into their enthusiasm and understanding of technology, we can use digital tools to enrich their learning and understanding, but beware of assuming that just because they are competent with technology they will find it easy to use Mathematics-specific tools.

Give students time to play around and get used to any software you want them to use in lessons. Start with really simple examples so that students don't have to worry too much about the Mathematics while they are getting to grips with the commands available to them. There is a great sense of achievement from solving even very simple problems if you are using a new tool to do it. A good introductory experience with a new tool will give students the confidence to try harder challenges without feeling anxious.

The following are some suggestions of very simple starting points for getting used to different digital tools:

Dynamic geometry

Draw:

- a line, a line segment, a ray – what's the difference?
- another line, parallel to your first line
- a square – and measure its side lengths
- other regular polygons – and measure their angles
- a circle – and measure its area
- a parallelogram, a trapezium, a kite
- a tessellation of regular polygons.

Encourage students to be playful, and not be anxious if they can't create something on their first attempt. Encourage them to move points around and get a feel for how the canvas changes, and how each part of the construction depends on the parts that went before.

Spreadsheets

- Generate a list of the natural numbers in column A.
- Create a list of even numbers in column B, by using a formula and dragging down.

- Use the SUM function to find the sum of the first 50 even numbers.
- Use the AVERAGE function to find the average of the first 50 even numbers.
- Generate a list of square numbers and plot them on a graph.

Graphing software or graphical calculators

- Plot the line $y = 2x + 4$.
- Plot some lines that cross the y axis in the same place.
- Plot some lines that are parallel to your first line.
- Plot some lines that are perpendicular to your first line.
- Plot some lines that cross the x axis in the same place.

Once students have had a chance to get to grips with a new digital tool, they can use it to work on a variety of interesting mathematical activities. The rest of this chapter explores the potential of these tools in a bit more detail, and suggests some engaging activities you might like to use in your classroom.

Dynamic geometry

Dynamic geometry has the potential to transform the way we teach Mathematics, and, with free web-based software available, anyone with access to a computer or tablet can try it out. A lesson on circle theorems without technology might involve students drawing some triangles in semicircles, noticing that one of the angles is always a right angle, and then coming up with, or being shown, a proof. Dynamic geometry allows students to create an example and then vary it to see what stays the same and what changes. It is much quicker to come up with geometric conjectures when you can generate many examples with a drag of the mouse!

Some teachers worry that dynamic geometry may take away the need for proof, which is at the heart of geometrical thinking. If students can see that a proposition is true for the examples on their screen, they may have no incentive to formally prove it. We disagree; the students who would be satisfied with seeing the truth in the examples on the screen would probably also be satisfied with drawing a few examples with a pencil and ruler. It is up to us as Mathematics teachers to help students understand the distinction between demonstration and proof, and give proof a higher status in our classrooms.

Here is an example where exploration with dynamic geometry software can lead to a conjecture. You may wish to create a dynamic diagram for yourself in order to explore.

In the diagram (Figure 11.2), the line BE bisects angle ABC, and the line CE bisects angle ACD.

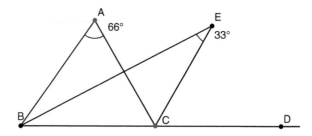

Figure 11.2

What do you notice about angles BAC and BEC as A moves? Can you prove your conjecture?

Spreadsheets

In the same way that we can use dynamic geometry to generate examples that lead to conjectures in geometry, we can also use spreadsheets for generating and testing conjectures for numerical problems. Consider the NRICH problem 'Generating Triples': (www.nrich.maths.org/generatingtriples), where students are challenged to find sets of numbers like 3, 4, 5 and 5, 12, 13 that satisfy the Pythagorean relationship $a^2 + b^2 = c^2$.

Students could begin by exploring on paper, but by using spreadsheets they can quickly search for patterns with much bigger numbers. Some students might notice that in the two Pythagorean triples above the two larger numbers differ by 1. Table 11.1 shows how such students might use a spreadsheet to find more Pythagorean triples of the form $a^2 + b^2 = (b + 1)^2$ by looking for square numbers in the third column.

b	b^2	$(b+1)^2 - b^2$
1	1	3
2	4	5
3	9	7
4	16	9
5	25	11
6	36	13
7	49	15
8	64	17
9	81	19
10	100	21
11	121	23
12	144	25
13	169	27
14	196	29
15	225	31

Table 11.1

Sometimes, dragging down a column in a spreadsheet and seeing results appear can provide a 'wow' moment as we see patterns that are worth exploring! We hope that students will notice that all of the numbers in the third column of the table are odd, and then start to speculate where the other odd square numbers will appear in the list. Even if your students don't have access to spreadsheets, using a calculator to explore numerical problems allows them to try more examples than they would be able to do by hand, making generalisations easier to spot.

Spreadsheets are not just useful for number work but can also be a powerful tool for teaching data handling. Many professional statisticians are surprised that school students still work with small data sets and calculate statistics by hand. In the world of work, most manipulations of data are automated. In the NRICH problem 'What's the Weather Like?' (www.nrich.maths.org/whatstheweatherlike), students are invited to download a spreadsheet containing weather data and come up with hypotheses that they can test. The spreadsheet has several hundred rows of data, in several columns. Analysing this data by hand would be time-consuming and would likely lead to mistakes, so instead, let students explore the different statistical functions that a spreadsheet can perform. As they become more practised at using the spreadsheet functions, they have more time to think deeply about what the statistics mean and how to interpret the data in relation to a hypothesis.

Graphing software and graphical calculators

Graphing software is another tool that students can use to look at many more examples than a paper and pencil method would allow. In the same way that dynamic geometry allows students to watch shapes transform and notice similarities and differences, graphing software allows them to transform functions, test ideas and gain insight into the relationship between graphs and equations.

☑ LESSON IDEA ONLINE 11.2: PARABOLIC PATTERNS

In the NRICH task 'Parabolic Patterns' (www.nrich.maths.org/parabolicpatterns), students are invited to use graphing software to recreate a pattern (Figure 11.3): →

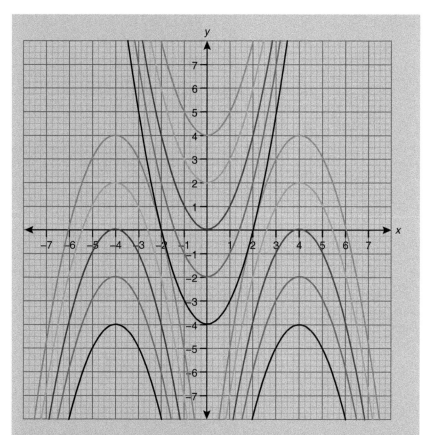

Figure 11.3

One of the curves is the graph of $y = x^2$, another has the equation $y = -(x - 4)^2$. How might students work out the equations of the other curves? One way would be to invite them to draw the given equations using graphing software, and then explore what happens as they change values in the equations. This allows them to seek for themselves the rules that govern transformations of functions. After they have had a chance to explore, bring the class together to discuss what they have found and formalise the rules they have discovered.

Next, invite students to design a similar pattern of their own and print it out. They can then challenge each other to figure out the equations of the graphs WITHOUT using the computer.

Teacher Tip

Graph sketching and transformations is a topic that many students struggle with. Allow them to use graphing software to be playful with graphs with the benefit of instant feedback, so they can develop the confidence to sketch curves when technology is unavailable.

Programming

In 1772, Leonhard Euler proved that 214748367 is prime, a feat that required him to perform 372 division calculations by hand. In the 21st century, a computer program a couple of lines long can demonstrate that 214748367 is prime in a fraction of a second! More and more jobs require students to be able to work with computers, and an understanding of how programs work can be valuable. Mathematics problems are a great motivation for doing some simple programming, as a program can quickly check lots of calculations that would take a very long time by hand. Writing programs requires very similar skills to those needed for mathematical reasoning and proof. If you miss a step in your logic, your program simply won't work, so encouraging students to program can exercise their mathematical muscles.

You could share with students the story of the 'Four Colour' theorem, one of the first mathematical theorems to be proved with the help of a computer, and the controversy surrounding whether or not it was an acceptable proof.

Teacher Tip

The cryptarithm problem TWO + TWO = FOUR mentioned in Chapter 8 **Metacognition** can be solved with the help of programs. You could encourage students to develop a program to help them find other examples of cryptarithms.

Here are some other examples of mathematical problems that can be solved by writing a program:

'Funny Factorisation' (www.nrich.maths.org/funnyfactorisation)

'Counting Factors' (www.nrich.maths.org/countingfactors)

'Shopping Basket' (www.nrich.maths.org/shoppingbasket)

Summary

You can use digital technology in the Mathematics classroom, not just as a tool for teacher demonstration, but also to allow students to explore much more than they otherwise could.

Make sure that your students get plenty of opportunities to use digital tools. Students need to experience the power of computers if they are to be prepared for the mathematical landscape they will meet when they leave school.

Many great lessons have no digital component at all. Save technology for situations where it really enriches your students' learning experience.

12 Global thinking

What is global thinking?

Global thinking is about learning how to live in a complex world as an active and engaged citizen. It is about considering the bigger picture and appreciating the nature and depth of our shared humanity.

When we encourage global thinking in students we help them recognise, examine and express their own and others' perspectives. We need to scaffold students' thinking to enable them to engage on cognitive, social and emotional levels, and construct their understanding of the world to be able to participate fully in its future.

We as teachers can help students develop routines and habits of mind to enable them to move beyond the familiar, discern that which is of local and global significance, make comparisons, take a cultural perspective and challenge stereotypes. We can encourage them to learn about contexts and traditions, and provide opportunities for them to reflect on their own and others' viewpoints.

Why adopt a global thinking approach?

Global thinking is particularly relevant in an interconnected, digitised world where ideas, opinions and trends are rapidly and relentlessly circulated. Students learn to pause and evaluate. They study why a topic is important on a personal, local and global scale, and they will be motivated to understand the world and their significance in it. Students gain a deeper understanding of why different viewpoints and ideas are held across the world.

Global thinking is something we can nurture both within and across disciplines. We can invite students to learn how to use different lenses from each discipline to see and interpret the world. They also learn how best to apply and communicate key concepts within and across disciplines. We can help our students select the appropriate media and technology to communicate and create their own personal synthesis of the information they have gathered.

Global thinking enables students to become more rounded individuals who perceive themselves as actors in a global context and who value diversity. It encourages them to become more aware, curious and interested in learning about the world and how it works. It helps students to challenge assumptions and stereotypes, to be better informed and more respectful. Global thinking takes the focus beyond exams and grades, or even checklists of skills and attributes. It develops students who are more ready to compete in the global marketplace and more able to participate effectively in an interconnected world.

What are the challenges of incorporating global thinking?

The pressures of an already full curriculum, the need to meet national and local standards, and the demands of exam preparation may make it seem challenging to find time to incorporate global thinking into lessons and programmes of study. A whole-school approach may be required for global thinking to be incorporated in subject plans for teaching and learning.

We need to give all students the opportunity to find their voice and participate actively and confidently, regardless of their background and world experiences, when exploring issues of global significance. We need to design suitable activities that are clear, ongoing and varying. Students need to be able to connect with materials, and extend and challenge their thinking. We also need to devise and use new forms of assessment that incorporate flexible and cooperative thinking.

Introduction

Many Mathematics teachers join the profession because they not only want to communicate their passion for Mathematics to others, but they also want a career that makes a difference, that makes the world a better place. We hope that our students will leave our schools with a sense of responsibility for their local, national and global communities, equipped with the mathematical tools they need to navigate their lives and shape the world around them. With wall-to-wall news coverage and new media, our students are more connected than ever before, and acutely aware of the challenges they will face as adults. Issues such as the environment, sustainability, and a rapidly growing world population matter to young people today more than ever before, and we need to show them where Mathematics fits into this bigger picture.

In a busy curriculum with pressure to deliver target grades, teaching Mathematics with a global perspective may feel like yet another extra to squeeze in. It doesn't have to be. If we want to embed global thinking in our Mathematics teaching, there are areas of the Mathematics curriculum where it is natural to do so. In the rest of the chapter, we suggest ways in which you can make your classroom a globally focused one.

The use and misuse of statistics

In this information age, we are bombarded with data. Just about every subject in the school curriculum has its own relevant data and representations, and the media is full of data, graphs, averages and predictions, used to persuade, convince, and sometimes manipulate us. As Mathematics teachers, it is up to us to ensure that our students can collect, process, represent and interpret data accurately and appropriately. We do not yet know which important issues our students will face in their lives, but we need to ensure that they leave school confident and competent at interpreting and analysing information so they are able to make good decisions.

When teaching new statistical techniques to our students, it can be tempting to stick to 'nice' numbers and relatively small datasets. However, this can be a missed opportunity – there are many exciting and engaging sources of data out there that can be used to fulfil a greater purpose than simply teaching a new skill.

Collecting data

Students need to be able to collect data for themselves and also research data from secondary sources. One motivation for their own data collection could be an issue of local importance – a proposed transport link, a new shopping centre, building wind turbines, or the closure of a public library, for example. Students could canvas opinion within the school and local community, and present their findings. Of particular interest may be whether different demographics within the population have very different opinions.

Here is an idea to get students thinking about bias in sampling. Split the class up into smaller groups and ask them to design a survey about shopping. Hand out briefing sheets, asking them to consider the questions they would ask, who they would choose to ask, and where they would go to conduct the survey. Don't mention that there are two versions of the briefing sheet! The first begins, 'You are conducting a survey for a group of small shop owners and want to know what type of shops people prefer', and the second says 'You are conducting a survey on behalf of a large supermarket chain, and want to know what type of shops people prefer'. When you bring the class together to share their suggestions, there will be outcry as each group hears the other group making the opposite suggestions to their own! Then you can reveal that the purpose of the survey was different for each group, to emphasise that we need to consider carefully who and what we ask if we want to gather unbiased results.

When teaching about secondary data, internet access opens up many possibilities for student research into subjects that interest them. Take, for example, the NRICH task 'Who's the Best?' (www.nrich.maths.org/ whosthebest) in which students are given a copy of the Olympic medal table and invited to answer the question:

- Which countries have the most naturally athletic populations?

Students need to consider the following questions:

- Does the Olympic table rank countries according to their natural athleticism?
- How might the population size of a nation affect its chances of winning a medal?
- What about the wealth of a nation?
- What other factors apart from natural athleticism might affect a country's ranking at the Olympics?

They will need to carry out research into the factors they identify, and could finish off the project by producing a new medal table based on their findings. (www.nrich.maths.org/whosthebest/solution) shows one student's analysis and his suggested medal table (in which Jamaica comes top of the table), which takes into account the population of each nation.

Teacher Tip

Bring examples from school politics into Maths lessons. Does your school have a student council? Teach the 'Handling Data' cycle by inviting students to research a topic they care about in their school life, collect some data, and then present their findings to their student representatives. Here are a few ideas on which students often have very strong opinions: school lunches, the provision of lockers and bike sheds, school uniforms, reward and punishment systems … the list goes on and on.

Representing data

As more media sources than ever before compete for our attention, data is presented to us in new and exciting ways. The NRICH problems 'Picturing the World' (www.nrich.maths.org/picturingtheworld) and 'Perception Versus Reality' (www.nrich.maths.org/perception) demonstrate some infographics and videos that have been used to represent data, particularly the idea of using visual images to represent very large data sets. In the book *If the World Were a Village*, David Smith and Shelagh

Armstrong imagine the world as a village of 100 people and show various world statistics in terms of the number of villagers. Stan's Café Theatre Company represented each person in the world as a single grain of rice, and then arranged them in heaps to help people compare different groups (www.stanscafe.co.uk/project-of-all-the-people.html#introduction). Why not show your students these ways to represent data and invite them to choose an innovative way to represent data that matters to them? One student made a video about the distribution of religions in England, (www.nrich.maths.org/perception/solution). You may wish to share it with your students to inspire them.

Teacher Tip

The Gapminder website (www.gapminder.org) is a great source of amazing data representations for a variety of important global issues. For example, there is a 'Bubble Chart' tool showing life expectancy plotted against GDP per capita animated over a 200-year period. Invite students to make predictions and then watch the animation to see whether their predictions are correct.

Interpreting data

'Going to University increases the risk of getting a brain tumour.'
'Heat-related deaths will rise 257% by 2050 because of climate change.'
'Just one glass of wine a week while pregnant "can harm a baby's IQ".'
'Shock warning: mobile phones can give you cancer.'

These four examples of sensationalist newspaper headlines don't quite reveal the full story! As well as interpreting data in their own statistical projects, our students will need to be critical about data that is presented to them, particularly in the media. The 'Understanding Uncertainty' website (www.understandinguncertainty.org) and the NHS 'Behind the Headlines' website (www.nhs.uk/News/Pages/NewsIndex.aspx) are good sources of news stories where, if you dig a little deeper, you find that newspapers sometimes oversimplify, misunderstand or misrepresent the research they are reporting.

The following is a classroom activity that might help students to engage with these issues. You and your students could choose some news stories and collect examples of how they have been reported by different news outlets. Here are some questions you could encourage your students to ask, to help them think critically about what appears in the articles:

• Has some information been omitted?
• Has the chart been drawn to accurately represent the situation?
• What do we know about the way the data was collected?
• How could we present the data more clearly and accurately?

Teacher Tip

As an ongoing project for your students, invite them to look out for occasions where statistics are used in the media. Every now and then, spend a lesson or two working on the examples that they find, together with some carefully chosen examples of your own, and create a classroom display focused on 'Bad Statistics'.

Dealing with risk and uncertainty

When we make decisions, we often have to weigh up the risks and benefits of each possible course of action. Probability allows us to use Mathematics to inform these decisions. Here are some ideas for helping students become more confident at applying their understanding of probability to real-world scenarios.

Medical tests sometimes give false positives (e.g. the test indicates that you have a disease when you are actually healthy) and false negatives (e.g. the test indicates that you are healthy when you actually have the disease). So, if you test positive, how likely is it you have the disease? To answer this question, we need to know about the rate at which the disease occurs in the population, and the accuracy of the test. This allows us to decide whether we should get tested, and if we do, how to interpret the results.

See the NRICH problem 'The ELISA test' (www.nrich.maths.org/elisa).

It is unlikely that you will win the lottery, and yet someone wins it almost every week. In a large enough population, coincidences and unlikely events are almost certain to happen somewhere, it's just that we can't predict who will be the lucky (or unlucky) person. For example, if 1000 people flip a coin ten times, it's reasonably likely that someone will get ten heads or tails in a row. If you are that person, you might feel very special, but we shouldn't be surprised that it happened to someone!

If a class of 30 students are invited to write down a secret number between 1 and 225, it might seem unlikely that two students would choose the same number, but it will happen more than 85% of the time! The NRICH problem 'Same Number' (www.nrich.maths.org/samenumber) explores the mathematics behind this unexpected result.

Sometimes it's useful to work in terms of frequencies rather than fractions or percentages, particularly when considering relative and absolute risk. For example, newspapers recently reported that the risk of bowel cancer increases by 20% if you eat meat every day. This suggests eating meat is a really bad idea! Is it?

Among people who do not have meat every day, around 5% will get bowel cancer. So, in a group of 100 people who do not eat much meat, we expect 5 people to get bowel cancer. If they all started eating meat every day, the risk increases by 20%, so instead of 5 people getting bowel cancer, 6 will. Does it still seem like such a bad idea to have meat every day? We can make better decisions if we know the absolute risk (1 extra person in 100) rather than the relative risk (20% increase). See the NRICH problem `How risky is my diet' (www.nrich.maths.org/risky) for some videos that you could share with students.

Global issues – collaborating with other subjects

Some of our students care passionately about global issues and feel frustrated that they can't influence politicians making decisions on the global stage. We can empower them by helping them to see how their own actions, however small, really do make a difference, both locally and globally. Although young people may feel that there is not much they can do, here are decisions they might be able to make for themselves:

- the food they eat
- the clothes they wear
- the way they get from place to place
- how they choose to spend their money
- how they choose to spend their free time.

It is not really our job as Mathematics teachers to give students background knowledge about topics such as sustainability, carbon footprints, energy efficiency, fair trade or activism, but it is important that we support our colleagues in other subjects who are introducing students to some of these issues. For example, if we know that students will be studying population growth in Geography, we can plan a lesson on exponential functions. If we know that students are working on packaging in Technology, we can plan a lesson on volume and surface area. Many global issues students meet in other subjects will require them to understand and work with very large numbers, so when we teach estimation and approximation we can use real-life examples:

- How much water is saved if we have a shower rather than a bath?
- How much energy would we save if we remembered to switch off lights whenever we leave the room?
- How does the carbon footprint of growing and transporting an apple compare with producing, packaging and transporting a bar of chocolate?

Questions such as these require students to do some research, make calculations and then justify their conclusions.

Teacher Tip

Make links with other subjects in the school. Find out when topics from Mathematics crop up in other lessons such as the humanities, sciences and social sciences, and liaise with other teachers to make connections.

Collaborate to change the world

It's not enough just to know about the world around us; we have to be able to work with others if we want to make the world a better place! Regardless of what students are learning, they can do much more together than alone. Earlier chapters have touched on the importance of collaborative working for effective learning in Mathematics. Collaboration supports students to become better mathematicians, and also helps them to develop into globally responsible citizens. Our students need to be able to listen to each other's ideas, appreciate that there are different ways of solving a problem, and value everyone's contribution.

One way to develop these skills in your classroom is to have the expectation that students work together to develop understanding and solve problems as a community. Here are some guiding principles that you may wish to establish with your class:

• Only one person speaks at a time.
• Everyone gets a chance to speak.
• Suggestions must never be ridiculed.
• Evidence and logical reasoning are used to resolve conflict and establish truth.

When students are working in groups, make it clear that it is everybody's responsibility to ensure that anyone in the group can report back on progress. When a group claims to have solved the problem, choose a student at random to explain their solution. If that student can't clearly explain and answer your questions, leave them to work together for a little longer until they can. This means that students can learn to communicate their reasoning effectively and to value ideas that are not their own. You can read about Jo Boaler's research on the benefits of collaborative work and raising achievement through group worthy tasks here: (www.nrich.maths.org/complexinstruction).

Dan Meyer's activity, 'Pyramid of Pennies', invites students to work out how many pennies there are in a pyramid (www.threeacts.mrmeyer.com/pyramidofpennies) The problem is based on a video that prompts students to ask questions that they can then work on in groups. Tasks like this encourage students to think mathematically, ask their own questions, and get used to perceiving the mathematics in new situations. These sorts of question are often too big to answer alone, so being part of a group that shares insights and approaches is really valuable.

Teacher Tip

Start a collection of video clips and images that might provoke mathematical questions. For example, you could show students a time lapse video of a house being built, and invite them to come up with mathematical questions such as 'How many bricks were needed?' or 'How many trees were cut down?'. Then, challenge students to do some research that allows them to answer their questions.

Summary

Students may feel that they cannot influence global issues, but issues of local importance offer a chance for them to make a difference. When teaching for global thinking, we can help students to consider global, local and individual issues and how they respond to each. Awareness of global issues gives them the motivation to try to influence local issues, and to make decisions for themselves on the issues that are closest to home. Even if your curriculum doesn't demand it, there are many benefits to using real-world examples to motivate and engage your students.

- Young people often have a keen sense of natural justice and an enthusiasm for learning about the world around them. If we can tap into this, we can help them appreciate the importance of Mathematics as a tool to understand the world and make decisions.

- Statistics offers a great opportunity to consider global thinking in Mathematics lessons. Invite students to analyse real-world examples based on issues that matter to them.

- Understanding probability, risk and uncertainty empowers students to make good decisions about many aspects of their lives.

- Mathematics goes on in other subjects too. Talk to teachers of other subjects and build cross-curricular links wherever possible.

- Nobody can save the world on their own, so collaboration is a vital skill for your students to learn. Model this in your classroom by inviting students to work together, encouraging robust discussion, and valuing everyone's contribution.

13

Reflective practice

Dr Paul Beedle, Head of Professional Development
Qualifications, Cambridge International Examinations

'As a teacher you are always learning'

It is easy to say this, isn't it? Is it true? Are you bound to learn just by being a teacher?

You can learn every day from the experience of working with your students, collaborating with your colleagues and playing your part in the life of your school. You can learn also by being receptive to new ideas and approaches, and by applying and evaluating these in practice in your own context.

To be more precise, let us say that as a teacher:

- You **should** always be learning
  to develop your expertise throughout your career for your own fulfilment as a member of the teaching profession and to be as effective as possible in the classroom.
- You **can** always be learning
  if you approach the teaching experience with an open mind, ready to learn and knowing how to reflect on what you are doing in order to improve.

You want your professional development activities to be as relevant as possible to what you do and who you are, and to help change the quality of your teaching and your students' learning – for the better, in terms of outcomes, and for good, in terms of lasting effect. You want to feel that 'it all makes sense' and that you are actively following a path that works for you personally, professionally and career-wise.

So professional learning is about making the most of opportunities and your working environment, bearing in mind who you are, what you are like and how you want to improve. But simply experiencing – thinking about and responding to situations, and absorbing ideas and information – is not necessarily learning. It is through reflection that you can make the most of your experience to deepen and extend your professional skills and understanding.

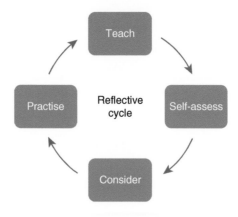

Figure 13.1

In this chapter, we will focus on three *essentials* of reflective practice, explaining in principle and in practice how you can support your own continuing professional development:

1 **Focusing** on what you want to learn about and why
2 **Challenging** yourself and others to go beyond description and assumptions to critical analysis and evaluation
3 **Sharing** what you are learning with colleagues – to enrich understanding and enhance the quality of practice.

These essentials will help you as you apply and adapt the rich ideas and approaches in this book in your own particular context. They will also help you if you are, or are about to be, taking part in a Cambridge Professional Development Qualification (Cambridge PDQ) programme, to make the most of your programme, develop your portfolio and gain the qualification.

1 Focus
In principle

Given the multiple dimensions and demands of being a teacher, you might be tempted to try to cover 'everything' in your professional development but you will then not have the time to go beneath the surface much at all. Likewise, attending many different training events will certainly keep you very busy but it is unlikely that these will simply add up to improving your thinking and practice in sustainable and systematic ways.

Teachers who are beginning an organised programme of professional learning find that it is most helpful to select particular ideas, approaches and topics which are relevant to their own situation and their school's priorities. They can then be clear about their professional learning goals, and how their own learning contributes to improving their students' learning outcomes. They deliberately choose activities that help make sense of their practice with their students in their school and have clear overall purpose.

It is one thing achieving focus, and another maintaining this over time. When the going gets tough, because it is difficult either to understand or become familiar with new ideas and practices, or to balance learning time with the demands of work and life, it really helps to have a mission – to know why you want to learn something as well as what that something is. Make sure that this is a purpose which you feel genuinely belongs to you and in which you have a keen interest, rather than it being something given to you or imposed on you. Articulate your focus not just by writing it down but by 'pitching' it to a colleague whose opinion you trust and taking note of their feedback.

In practice

- Plan
  What is my goal and how will I approach the activity?

  Select an approach that is new to you, but make sure that you understand the thinking behind this and that it is relevant to your students' learning. Do it for real effect, not for show.

- Monitor
  Am I making progress towards my goal; do I need to try a different approach?

  Take time during your professional development programme to review how far and well you are developing your understanding of theory and practice. What can you do to get more out of the experience, for example by discussing issues with your mentor, researching particular points, and asking your colleagues for their advice?

- Evaluate
  What went well, what could have been better, what have I learned for next time?

  Evaluation can sometimes be seen as a 'duty to perform' – like clearing up after the event – rather than the pivotal moment in learning that it really is. Evaluate not because you are told you have to; evaluate to make sense of the learning experience you have been through and what it means to you, and to plan ahead to see what you can do in the future.

This cycle of planning, monitoring and evaluation is just as relevant to you as a professional learner as to your students as learners. Be actively in charge of your learning and take appropriate actions. Make your professional development work for you. Of course your professional development programme leaders, trainers and mentors will guide and support you in your learning, but you are at the heart of your own learning experience, not on the receiving end of something that is cast in stone. Those who assist and advise you on your professional development want you and your colleagues to get the best out of the experience, and need your feedback along the way so that if necessary they can adapt and improve what they are devising.

2 Challenge

In principle

Reflection is a constructive process that helps the individual teacher to improve their thinking and practice. It involves regularly asking questions of yourself about your developing ideas and experience, and keeping track of your developing thinking, for example in a reflective journal. Reflection is continuous, rather than a one-off experience. Being honest with yourself means thinking hard, prompting yourself to go beyond your first thoughts about a new experience and to avoid taking for granted your opinions about something to which you are accustomed. Be a critical friend to yourself.

In the Cambridge PDQ Certificate in Teaching and Learning, for example, teachers take a fresh look at the concepts and processes of learning and challenge their own assumptions. They engage with theory and models of effective teaching and learning, and open their minds through observing experienced practitioners, applying new ideas in practice and listening to formative feedback from mentors and colleagues. To evidence in their assessed portfolio how they have learned from this experience, they not only present records of observed practice but also critical analysis showing understanding of how and why practices work and how they can be put into different contexts successfully.

The Cambridge PDQ syllabuses set out key questions to focus professional learning and the portfolio templates prompts to help you. These questions provide a framework for reflection. They are open-ended and will not only stimulate your thinking but lead to lively group discussion. The discipline of asking yourself and others questions such as 'Why?' 'How do we know?' 'What is the evidence?' 'What are the conditions?' leads to thoughtful and intelligent practice.

In practice

Challenge:

- Yourself, as you reflect on an experience, to be more critical in your thinking. For example, rather than simply describing what happened, analyse why it happened and its significance, and what might have happened if conditions had been different.
- Theory – by understanding and analysing the argument, and evaluating the evidence that supports the theory. Don't simply accept a theory as a given fact – be sure that you feel that the ideas make sense and that there is positive value in applying them in practice.
- Convention – the concept of 'best practice(s)' is as good as we know now, on the basis of the body of evidence, for example on the effect size of impact of a particular approach on learning outcomes. By using an approach in an informed way and with a critical eye, you can evaluate the approach relating to your particular situation.

3 Share

In principle

Schools are such busy places, and yet teachers can feel they are working on their own for long periods because of the intensity of their workload as they focus on all that is involved in teaching their students. We know that a crucial part of our students' active learning is the opportunity to collaborate with their peers in order to investigate, create and communicate. Just so with professional learning: teachers learn best through engagement with their peers, in their own school and beyond. Discussion and interaction with colleagues, focused on learning and student outcomes, and carried out in a culture of openness, trust and respect, helps each member of the community of practice in the school clarify and sharpen their understanding and enhance their practice.

This is why the best professional learning programmes incorporate collaborative learning, and pivotal moments are designed into the programme for this to happen frequently over time: formally in guided learning sessions such as workshops and more informally in opportunities such as study group, teach meets and discussion, both face-to-face and online.

Approaches to learning and teaching Mathematics

In practice

Go beyond expectations!

In the Cambridge PDQ syllabus, each candidate needs to carry out an observation of an experienced practitioner and to be observed formatively themselves by their mentor on a small number of occasions. This is the formal requirement in terms of evidence of practice within the portfolio for the qualification. The expectation is that these are not the only times that teachers will observe and be observed for professional learning purposes (rather than performance appraisal).

However, the more that teachers can observe each other's teaching, the better; sharing of practice leads to advancement of shared knowledge and understanding of aspects of teaching and learning, and development of agreed shared 'best practice'.

So:

- open your classroom door to observation
- share with your closest colleague(s) when you are trying out a fresh approach, for example an idea in this book
- ask them to look for particular aspects in the lesson, especially how students are engaging with the approach – pose an observation question
- reflect with them after the lesson on what you and they have learned from the experience – pose an evaluation question
- go and observe them as they do the same
- after a number of lessons, discuss with your colleagues how you can build on your peer observation with common purpose, for example lesson study
- share with your other colleagues in the school what you are gaining from this collaboration and encourage them to do the same
- always have question(s) to focus observations and focus these question(s) on student outcomes.

Pathways

The short-term effects of professional development are very much centred on teachers' students. For example, the professional learning in a Cambridge PDQ programme should lead directly and quickly to changes in the ways your students learn. All teachers have this at heart – the desire to help their students learn better.

The long-term effects of professional development are more teacher-centric. During their career over, say, 30 years, a teacher may teach many thousand lessons. There are many good reasons for a teacher to keep up-to-date with pedagogy, not least to sustain their enjoyment of what they do.

Each teacher will follow their own career pathway, taking into account many factors. We do work within systems, at school and wider level, involving salary and appointment levels, and professional development can be linked to these as requirement or expectation. However, to a significant extent teachers shape their own career pathway, making decisions along the way. Their pathway is not pre-ordained; there is room for personal choice, opportunity and serendipity. It is for each teacher to judge for themselves how much they wish to venture. A teacher's professional development pathway should reflect and support this.

It is a big decision to embark on an extended programme of professional development, involving a significant commitment of hours of learning and preparation over several months. You need to be as clear as you can be about the immediate and long-term value of such a commitment. Will your programme lead to academic credit as part of a stepped pathway towards Masters level, for example?

Throughout your career, you need to be mindful of the opportunities you have for professional development. Gauge the value of options available at each particular stage in your professional life, both in terms of relevance to your current situation – your students, subject and phase focus, and school – and the future situation(s) of which you are thinking.

14 Understanding the impact of classroom practice on student progress

Lee Davis, Deputy Director for Education, Cambridge International Examinations

Introduction

Throughout this book, you have been encouraged to adopt a more active approach to teaching and learning and to ensure that formative assessment is embedded into your classroom practice. In addition, you have been asked to develop your students as meta-learners, such that they are able to, as the academic Chris Watkins puts it, 'narrate their own learning' and become more reflective and strategic in how they plan, carry out and then review any given learning activity.

A key question remains, however. How will you know that the new strategies and approaches you intend to adopt have made a significant difference to your students' progress and learning? What, in other words, has been the impact and how will you know?

This chapter looks at how you might go about determining this at the classroom level. It deliberately avoids reference to whole-school student tracking systems, because these are not readily available to all schools and all teachers. Instead, it considers what you can do as an individual teacher to make the learning of your students visible – both to you and anyone else who is interested in how they are doing. It does so by introducing the concept of 'effect sizes' and shows how these can be used by teachers to determine not just whether an intervention works or not but, more importantly, *how well* it works. 'Effect size' is a useful way of quantifying or measuring the size of any difference between two groups or data sets. The aim is to place emphasis on the most important aspect of an intervention or change in teaching approach – the **size of the effect** on student outcomes.

Consider the following scenario:

Over the course of a term, a teacher has worked hard with her students on understanding 'what success looks like' for any given task or activity. She has stressed the importance of everyone being clear about the criteria for success, before students embark upon the chosen task and plan their way through it. She has even got to the point where students have been co-authors of the assessment rubrics used, so that they have been fully engaged in the intended outcomes throughout and can articulate what is required before they have even started. The teacher is happy with developments so far, but has it made a difference to student progress? Has learning increased beyond what we would normally expect for an average student over a term anyway?

Here is an extract from the teacher's markbook.

Student	Sept Task	Nov Task
Katya	13	15
Maria	15	20
Joao	17	23
David	20	18
Mushtaq	23	25
Caio	25	38
Cristina	28	42
Tom	30	35
Hema	32	37
Jennifer	35	40

Figure 14.1

Before we start analysing this data, we must note the following:

- The task given in September was at the start of the term – the task in November was towards the end of the term.
- Both tasks assessed similar skills, knowledge and understanding in the student.
- The maximum mark for each was 50.
- The only variable that has changed over the course of the term is the approaches to teaching and learning by the teacher. All other things are equal.

With that in mind, looking at Figure 14.1, what conclusions might you draw as an external observer?

You might be saying something along the lines of: 'Mushtaq and Katya have made some progress, but not very much. Caio and Cristina appear to have done particularly well. David, on the other hand, appears to be going backwards!'

What can you say about the class as a whole?

Calculating effect sizes

What if we were to apply the concept of 'effect sizes' to the class results in Figure 14.1, so that we could make some more definitive statements about the impact of the interventions over the given time period? Remember, we are doing so in order to understand the size of the effect on student outcomes or progress.

Let's start by understanding how it is calculated.

An effect size is found by calculating 'the standardised mean difference between two data sets or groups'. In essence, this means we are looking for the difference between two averages, while taking into the account the spread of values (in this case, marks) around those averages at the same time.

As a formula, and from Figure 14.1, it looks like the following:

$$\text{Effect size} = \frac{\text{average class mark (after intervention)} - \text{average class mark (before intervention)}}{\text{spread (standard deviation of the class)}}$$

In words: the average mark achieved by the class *before* the teacher introduced her intervention strategies is taken away from the average mark achieved by the class *after* the intervention strategies. This is then divided by the standard deviation[1] of the class as a whole.

---

[1] The standard deviation is merely a way of expressing by how much the members of a group (in this case, student marks in the class) differ from the average value (or mark) for the group.

Approaches to learning and teaching Mathematics

Inserting our data into a spreadsheet helps us calculate the effect size as follows:

	A	B	C
1	Student	September Task	November Task
2	Katya	13	15
3	Maria	15	20
4	Joao	17	23
5	David	20	18
6	Mushtaq	23	25
7	Caio	25	38
8	Cristina	28	42
9	Tom	30	35
10	Hema	32	37
11	Jennifer	35	40
12			
13	Average mark	23.8 = AVERAGE (B2:B11)	29.3 = AVERAGE (C2:C11)
14	Standard deviation	7.5 = STDEV (B2:B11)	10.11 = STDEV (C2:C11)

Figure 14.2

Therefore, the effect size for this class $= \dfrac{29.3 - 23.8}{8.8} = 0.62$
But what does this mean?

Interpreting effect sizes for classroom practice

In pure statistical terms, a 0.62 effect size means that the average student mark **after** the intervention by the teacher, is 0.62 standard deviations above the average student mark **before** the intervention.

We can state this in another way: the post-intervention average mark now exceeds 61% of the student marks previously.

Going further, we can also say that the average student mark, post-intervention, would have placed a student in the top four in the class previously. You can see this visually in Figure 14.2 where 29.3 (the class average after the teacher's interventions) would have been between Cristina's and Tom's marks in the September task.

This is good, isn't it? As a teacher, would you be happy with this progress by the class over the term?

To help understand effect sizes further, and therefore how well or otherwise the teacher has done above, let us look at how they are used in large-scale studies as well as research into educational effectiveness more broadly. We will then turn our attention to what really matters – talking about student learning.

Effect sizes in research

We know from results analyses of the Program for International Student Assessment (PISA) and the Trends in International Mathematics and Science Study (TIMMS) that, across the world, a year's schooling leads to an effect size of 0.4. John Hattie and his team at The University of Melbourne reached similar conclusions when looking at over 900 meta-analyses of classroom and whole-school interventions to improve student learning – 240 million students later, the result was an effect size of 0.4 on average for all these strategies.

What this means, then, is that any teacher achieving an effect size of greater than 0.4 is doing better than expected (than the average) over the course of a year. From our example above, not only are the students making better than expected progress, they are also doing so in just one term.

Here is something else to consider. In England, the distribution of GCSE grades in Maths and English have standard deviations of between 1.5 and 1.8 grades (A*, A, B, C, etc.), so an improvement of one GCSE grade represents an effect size of between 0.5 and 0.7. This means that, in the context of secondary schools, introducing a change in classroom practice of 0.62 (as the teacher achieved above) would result in an improvement of about one GCSE grade for each student in the subject.

Furthermore, for a school in which 50% of students were previously attaining five or more A*–C grades, this percentage (assuming the effect size of 0.62 applied equally across all subjects and all other things being equal) the percentage would rise to 73%.

Now, that's something worth knowing.

What next for your classroom practice? Talking about student learning

Given what we now know about effect sizes, what might be the practical next steps for you as a teacher?

Firstly, try calculating effect sizes for yourself, using marks and scores for your students that are comparable, e.g. student performance on key skills in maths, reading, writing, science practicals, etc. Become familiar with how they are calculated so that you can then start interrogating them 'intelligently'.

Do the results indicate progress was made? If so, how much is attributable to the interventions you have introduced?

Try calculating effect sizes for each individual student, in addition to your class, to make their progress visible too. To help illustrate this, let us return to the comments we were making about the progress of some students in Figure 14.1. We thought Cristina and Caio did very well and we had grave concerns about David. Individual effect sizes for the class of students would help us shed light on this further:

Student	September Task	November task	Individual Effect Size
Katya	13	15	0.22*
Maria	15	20	0.55
Joao	17	23	0.66
David	20	18	-0.22
Mushtaq	23	25	0.22
Caio	25	38	1.43
Cristina	28	42	1.54
Tom	30	35	0.55
Hema	32	37	0.55
Jennifer	35	40	0.55

* The individual effect size for each student above is calculated by taking their September mark away from their November mark and then dividing by the standard deviation for the class – in this case 8.8.

Figure 14.3

If these were your students, what questions would you now ask of yourself, of your students and even of your colleagues, to help you understand why the results are as they are and how learning is best achieved? Remember, an effect size of 0.4 is our benchmark, so who is doing better than that? Who is not making the progress we would expect?

David's situation immediately stands out, doesn't it? A negative effect size implies learning has regressed. So, what has happened, and how will we draw alongside him to find out what the issues are and how best to address them?

Why did Caio and Cristina do so well, considering they were just above average previously? Effect sizes of 1.43 and 1.54 respectively are significantly above the benchmark, so what has changed from their perspective? Perhaps they responded particularly positively to developing assessment rubrics together. Perhaps learning had sometimes been a mystery to them before, but with success criteria now made clear, this obstacle to learning had been removed.

We don't know the answers to these questions, but they would be great to ask, wouldn't they? So go ahead and ask them. Engage in dialogue with your students, and see how their own ability to discuss their learning has changed and developed. This will be as powerful a way as any of discovering whether your new approaches to teaching and learning have had an impact and it ultimately puts data, such as effect sizes, into context.

Concluding remarks

Effect sizes are a very effective means of helping you understand the impact of your classroom practice upon student progress. If you change your teaching strategies in some way, calculating effect sizes, for both the class and each individual student, helps you determine not just *if* learning has improved, but by *how much*.

They are, though, only part of the process. As teachers, we must look at the data carefully and intelligently in order to understand 'why'. Why did some students do better than others? Why did some not make any progress at all? Use effect sizes as a starting point, not the end in itself.

Ensure that you don't do this in isolation – collaborate with others and share this approach with them. What are your colleagues finding in their classes, in their subjects? Are the same students making the same progress across the curriculum? If there are differences, what might account for them?

In answering such questions, we will be in a much better position to determine next steps in the learning process for students. After all, isn't that our primary purpose as teachers?

Acknowledgements, further reading and resources

This chapter has drawn extensively on the influential work of the academics John Hattie and Robert Coe. You are encouraged to look at the following resources to develop your understanding further:

Hattie, J. (2012). *Visible Learning for Teachers – Maximising Impact on Learning.* London and New York: Routledge.

Coe, R. (2002). *It's the Effect Size, Stupid. What effect size is and why it is important.* Paper presented at the Annual Conference of The British Educational Research Association, University of Exeter, England, 12–14 September, 2002. A version of the paper is available online on the University of Leeds website.

The Centre for Evaluation and Monitoring, University of Durham, has produced a very useful effect size calculator (available from their website). Note that it also calculates a confidence interval for any effect size generated. Confidence intervals are useful in helping you understand the margin for error of an effect size you are reporting for your class. These are particularly important when the sample size is small, which will inevitably be the case for most classroom teachers.

15 Recommended reading

The resources in this section can be used as a supplement to your learning, to build upon your understanding of Mathematics teaching and the pedagogical themes in this series.

For a deeper understanding of the Cambridge approach, refer to the Cambridge International Examinations website (www. cie.org.uk/teaching-and-learning) where you will find the following in-depth guides:

Implementing the curriculum with Cambridge; a guide for school leaders.

Developing your school with Cambridge; a guide for school leaders.

Education briefs for a number of topics, such as active learning and bilingual education. Each brief includes information about the challenges and benefits of different approaches to teaching, practical tips, lists of resources.

Getting started with... These are interactive resources to help to explore and develop areas of teaching and learning. They include practical examples, reflective questions, and experiences from teachers and researchers.

For further support around becoming a Cambridge school visit Cambridge-community.org.uk.

This collection of articles identifies the key ideas and beliefs that have informed the development of NRICH resources:

NRICH Project, 'What we think and why we think it': www.nrich.maths.org/whatwethink, Cambridge: University of Cambridge.

This collection of articles offers suggestions on using rich tasks in the classroom:

NRICH Project, 'Enriching the Secondary Curriculum': www.nrich.maths.org/enriching. Cambridge: University of Cambridge.

This book unpicks what it means to think like a mathematician:

Mason, J., Leone Burton, L. and Stacey, K. (2010) *Thinking mathematically*. Harlow: Pearson.

15 Approaches to learning and teaching Mathematics

This book offers practical advice on helping all learners enjoy and succeed at mathematics:

Boaler, J. (2015). *Mathematical Mindsets: Unleashing students' potential through creative math, inspiring messages and innovative teaching.* John Wiley & Sons.

This short booklet offers insights gained by teachers who implemented key theoretical ideas in their classrooms:

Watson, A., De Geest, E. and Prestage, S. (2003) *Deep Progress in Mathematics - The Improving Attainment in Mathematics Project* www.pmtheta.com/uploads/4/7/7/8/47787337/deep_progress_book_2003.pdf, Oxford: University of Oxford, Department of Educational Studies.

This report introduces the strands of mathematical proficiency and offers suggestions on how to teach in a way that strengthens all the strands:

Kilpatrick, J. Swafford, J. and Findell, B. (editors) (2001), *Adding it up: Helping Children Learn Mathematics.* Mathematics Learning Study Committee, National Research Council: www.nap.edu/read/9822/chapter/1, Washington, DC: National Academy Press.

The following book draws attention to the value of having a growth mindset and what teachers can do to develop their students' potential:

Dweck, C. (2012), *Mindset: How you can fulfill your potential.* London: Constable and Robinson.

A valuable resource for extra reading on meta-learning in diverse classroom environments:

Watkins C (2015) *Meta-Learning in Classrooms.* The SAGE Handbook of Learning. Edited by Scott D. and Hargreaves E. London: Sage Publications Ltd.

Index

Approaches to learning and teaching Mathematics